CONTENTS

INTRODUCTION

On the evening of July 2, 2000, victory parties across Mexico were just getting under way as the long-ruling Institutional Revolutionary Party (PRI) prepared to celebrate another *sexenio* (six-year term) at the helm of Latin America's second most populous nation.

The PRI had ruled the country since the end of the 1910 Mexican Revolution, using a combination of political cunning, coercion, patronage, and sometimes outright fraud to win every presidential election it fought. It had little reason to think it might lose this one – although it was the first to be held under new rules that guaranteed a competitive and fair vote.

But as the early results trickled in, the merriment died away and a stunned disbelief set in. The party that had governed Mexico for 71 years as "the perfect dictatorship" had been ousted from office by an unlikely political force: a flamboyant former Coca-Cola executive and rancher named Vicente Fox Quesada, candidate of the center-right opposition National Action Party (PAN). Mexicans could barely believe their eyes when, a short time later, outgoing President Ernesto Zedillo appeared on national television to concede defeat.

Fox's simple campaign slogan – *ya!* (enough!) – summed up the aspirations of millions of Mexicans weary of the poverty, corruption and misrule they increasingly associated with the PRI. His victory marked the first peaceful transfer of power to the opposition in Mexico's often turbulent history, an event on a par with the death of General Franco in Spain and the end of apartheid in South Africa.

With over 97 million people, Mexico is the largest Spanish-speaking country in the world. Under the PRI, it was often seen in Washington as a troublesome neighbor, a source of drugs, illegal immigrants, and instability. But the newly democratic Mexico is being embraced as never before by both the new US president, George W. Bush, and by the Congress. As the United States' second-largest trading partner, Mexico's strategic importance is on the rise.

The PRI has left Mexico a decidedly mixed legacy. On the one hand, the party presided over decades of political stability and economic progress that made it the envy of Latin America. Since it joined Canada and the United States in the North American Free Trade Agreement (NAFTA) in 1994, it has become a growing manufacturing hub for automobiles, electronics, and industrial goods. Many of the biggest Mexican companies are multinationals in their own right, and the gleaming skyscrapers and corporate offices of Mexico City, Guadalajara, and Monterrey testify to a modern, first-world nation. Exports of music, films, pop stars, and

Students demonstrate in protest against tuition fees and neoliberalism *(Chris Sharp/South American Pictures)*

telenovelas (soap operas) have brought Mexican popular culture to vast audiences in North America, Europe, and Asia, and its universities and cultural institutions are among the largest and most important in Latin America.

But the PRI also presided over a series of six year-long economic crises, beginning in the late 1970s, which mired millions of Mexicans in poverty and left the country deeply in debt. Drug trafficking, official corruption, soaring crime, and the government's ineffectual handling of the 1985 Mexico City earthquake left the PRI increasingly discredited in the eyes of many Mexicans.

The PRI bequeathed an economic system with some of the worst income disparities in the world. Although Mexico is the only Latin American country that is a member of the OECD club of wealthy industrialized countries, it has levels of poverty, child mortality, malnutrition, and under-education on a par with the continent's poorest nations, such as Nicaragua and El Salvador. Some 40 million people live on less than $3 a day, scratching out a living in remote sierras and deserts and vast shantytowns of what anthropologist Guillermo Bonfil calls *Mexico Profundo* (Deep Mexico).

The Zapatista rebellion in the southern state of Chiapas reminded Mexicans and the world that the country's 8.7 million Amerindians – who constitute roughly half of Latin America's surviving indigenous people – live in almost feudal misery. And yet Mexico has more billionaires (thirteen) than any other country in the region, and a highly stratified class system that makes social mobility almost impossible for the largely mestizo and indigenous underclass.

Under PRI rule, Mexico had the trappings – an elected legislature, a nominally independent judiciary, a federal system, a liberal constitution – but not the substance of democratic life. The belated arrival of true pluralistic government has awakened hopes that Mexico might finally tackle the legcies of poverty and misrule that have held back this emerging giant of a nation for so long.

1   THE LAND

Borders

Under cover of darkness, undocumented workers slip into the river water and strike out for the other side. The scene is repeated every night on both Mexico's southern and northern borders.

The southern border with Guatemala and Belize snakes through the sparsely populated jungles and swamps of Chiapas, Tabasco, and Quintana Roo. By contrast, the 1,964-mile northern frontier is heavily patrolled by US immigration agents. Mexico's northern border constitutes the longest – and perhaps the only – land border between the first and the third world.

These two frontiers define a geopolitical quandary that dogs Mexican history. Is it the northernmost nation of Latin America or the most southern outpost of the North American mainland?

The busiest crossings on the southern border are along the Suchiate River, south of Tapachula, Chiapas. While long lines of trucks queue up at Tecún Umán, Guatemalans and other Central Americans illegally cross the river on inflated tire inner tubes. Some are escaping tyranny farther south (but Chinese and east Indians utilize this jumping off point too). Many are economic refugees seeking a better life farther north. Some will stay in Mexico but most will try to continue north into the United States. About 400,000 legal and undocumented Central Americans live in Mexico, 45 percent of them Guatemalan, including 50,000 contract coffee pickers and a diminishing population of recognized political refugees.

Undocumented workers from the south move carefully through Mexico. Immigration and police agents are notorious for extorting pay-offs as the newcomers pass through highway checkpoints and big city bus terminals. An unwritten agreement forged between former presidents George Bush and Carlos Salinas to shut down Mexico as a conduit for Central Americans heading toward the US, resulted in a crackdown by Mexico's own Immigration Service – over 100,000 Central Americans are now returned from Mexico to their countries of origin each year.

As Central Americans travel from border to border, they join a great stream of Mexicans seeking to reach *el otro lado* (the other side). Mexicans have been going north to make their fortune or escape political persecution since California and Texas were part of their country (they were gobbled up by the US in 1848).

The number of Mexicans heading for *el norte* peaks whenever political and economic upheaval troubles the republic. Mexican-American (*chicano*) communities in the US southwest were established by refugees fleeing the 1910–1917 revolution; the 1982 debt crisis is thought to have

Illegal imigrants crossing the Rio Grande between Ciudad Juárez and El Paso, Texas

(Julio Etchart/ Reportage)

pushed a million Mexican citizens into the United States. By 2001, some 3 million of the 8.5 million Mexican-born people living in the United States are illegal residents.

The presence of the US Border Patrol (*la migra*) makes the northern border a flashpoint between the two countries. Since 1994, when the Clinton administration launched Operation Gatekeeper to staunch the flow, parts of the border have been marked by steel fences, lights, and ground sensors. But the main effect of Clinton's beefed-up border surveillance has been to re-direct the flow of migrants through less settled and thus more dangerous crossing points, where they are more vulnerable to death from exposure.

In 2000, the *migra* made 1.6 million apprehensions – many would-be border jumpers were apprehended several times, often aided by *coyotes* (smugglers). Once dominated by small-time operators who worked independently, migrant smuggling has become a multi-billion dollar industry dominated by large, well-organized crime syndicates – rather like the drug business – using the tools of high technology and an infrastructure that includes drop houses where immigrants can be kept against their will until they pay off smugglers' fees. Increasingly, non-Mexicans are also using the Mexican border to enter the United States illegally. Thousands of Russians, Syrians, Chinese, and Poles are among those apprehended by the *migra* every year.

Mexicologists characterize the flow of undocumented workers into the US as a "safety valve" that permits Mexico to prevent the social frustrations of young Mexicans unable to find work from becoming a volatile challenge to their government. For decades of PRI rule, the Mexican government turned a blind eye to their plight – the deaths of migrants from drowning, exposure, and vigilante attacks on the US border; the harassment and extortion of returning migrants by corrupt Mexican border officials; and the high transaction costs paid by migrants sending home remittances to their families in Mexico, worth $8 billion a year.

Slums in Ciudad Juárez are home to thousands of employees of the *maquiladoras* factories on the Mexican-US border *(Julio Etchart/ Reportage)*

Indeed, these *paisanos* (countrymen) were often stigmatized by the Mexican state for supposed lack of patriotism for having left their homeland.

In contrast, the Fox government has actively courted the Mexican diaspora, promising them dual citizenship and setting up the country's first cabinet-level agency to represent their interests, the Office for Migrants Living Abroad. One of its most controversial proposals is to provide a survival kit – known informally as a *cajita feliz*, or "happy meal" – to each illegal migrant, in order to reduce the risk of death from exposure and thirst.

Anti-Mexican sentiment ebbed and flowed on the US side of the border in accordance with the need for low-wage Mexican labor. Mexicans were deported from California during the 1930s depression but were welcomed back in the 1940s to replace US workers who had gone off to war. The 1990s saw a resurgence of anti-Mexican feeling, reaching a zenith with the 1994 campaign for Proposition 187, the anti-illegal-immigrant ballot initiative in California.

But the election of George W. Bush in 2000 brought into office a strongly pro-Mexico US leader who had befriended Fox when both were still state governors. Even conservative Republicans in Congress were rushing to embrace the new Mexican president, promising initiatives to open the border to a freer flow of guest workers to the United States and a partial amnesty for illegals already there.

But Mexico's borders are not just escape hatches into the US for impoverished *indocumentados*. A cornucopia of goods, both legal and contraband, thunders across the border crossings. Since NAFTA was signed in 1994, Mexico–US trade has grown by 20 percent a year, reaching $248 billion worth of merchandise and services in 2000 – most of it passing by rail and road over the well-worn infrastructure of the northern border.

One major source of this movement are the *maquiladoras* or foreign-owned assembly plants that line the Mexican side. The maquiladoras are magnets for the underemployed from all over Mexico, especially the impoverished central and southern states. The surge of export-driven economic growth since NAFTA has created labor shortages and rising wages in parts of northern and central Mexico, forcing newer factories to locate in the poorer southern states of Yucatán, Guerrero, and Chiapas.

The North

With its enormous expanses of desert, grazing lands, grain fields, sky, and central *cordillera*, the north of Mexico could swallow up entire Latin American nations.

The seven states that comprise the north – Baja California North and South, Sonora, Durango, Chihuahua, Coahuila, Nuevo León, and Tamaulipas – stretch over half the Mexican map (Chihuahua is the largest state in the Mexican union).

The narrow, industrialized strip of the border marks the region's northern rim, concentrating the population around Tijuana, Ciudad Juárez, Nuevo Laredo, and Matamoros. These once forgotten outposts, located thousands of miles from the capital of the country, were built up in the 1930s by President Lázaro Cárdenas to fortify Mexican nationalism in a region where US influences are strong.

Today, 75 percent of the population of the north lives in towns and cities. The magnet cities along the northern frontier, besieged by migrants from the south, are straining at the seams. A lack of infrastructure and unenforced environmental regulations have resulted in groundwater contamination, dangerous pollution levels in border rivers, and deteriorating air quality. In Tijuana and other border hotspots, armies of pickers descend daily upon municipal garbage dumps to scratch out a living. Sprawling, unpaved shantytowns without basic services like sewers and running water bring the third world to the doorstep of the first.

Although an environmental accord attached to NAFTA promises a clean-up, by the second year of the treaty's life, few projects had yet been funded by the NAFTA-created North American Development Bank. Nonetheless, the concept of the border as an integrated bio-region, the responsibility for which is jointly shared by the US and Mexico, has taken root all along this northernmost fringe of the nation.

The desert is the region's most distinguishing feature. The Sonora desert extends into Arizona and the high Chihuahua desert spreads north into New Mexico and Texas. The eastern and western arms of the central cordillera march south down Mexico's spine, shaping *sierras* (mountain ranges) and deep gorges such as Copper Canyon, even deeper than the US Grand Canyon. The world's eighth largest copper pit is gouged from the earth at Cananea in Sonora. But it is manufacturing, not natural resources, that is increasingly the linchpin of the northern economy.

Wealth in the Mexican North is never very far from the surface of the land. The once-dense forests of the Tarahumara sierra (Chihuahua–Durango) have been thinned by timber interests – the Hearst family publishing fortune was nurtured by Tarahumara concessions, ceded by the dictator Porfirio Díaz.

The wealth of the region has fostered immense fortunes, nowhere more than in Monterrey, Mexico's third largest city (3.5 million). With its shining skyscrapers and modernistic museums, Monterrey has as much in common with the petrolopolises of Texas as it does with the capital of its own country. The Monterrey Group, the city's elite bankers and industrialists, exemplified by the Garza Sada dynasty (breweries, chemicals, glass) are major players in Mexico's economy.

The North is often viewed as a separate nation and the region's indigenous origins underscore this separateness. Most northern Indian cultures are grouped together under the Chichimeca rubric and are more closely related to Native American cultures of the US southwest than the predominant Nahuatl speakers of central Mexico. Ironically the Aztecs, who built their capital in the center of the country, had their origin in the Chichimeca culture of the north–central coastal state of Nayarit.

The European conquest of the north was never complete. The Yaquis of the Sonora desert fought on into the 20th century – Porfirio Díaz shipped thousands of captured Indian rebels south to the Yucatán jungles in 1907 in an effort to break their resistance.

The rebellious spirit of the northern frontier has not been limited to Indian uprisings. The 1910 revolution began in the north under the guiding hand of Francisco Madero. Doroteo Arango, also known as Francisco ("Pancho") Villa, the revolutionary leader from Chihuahua championed in the US by the journalist John Reed, was called "the Centaur of the North."

Despite its legacy as the cradle of revolution, political opposition in the North has most recently taken a conservative tilt: for over fifteen years, the right-of-center National Action Party (PAN) has challenged the PRI in regional elections, winning control of many state-houses and municipalities.

Central Mexico

Each year on the (usually rainy) evening of September 15, the plaza of Dolores Hidalgo, a sleepy town in the foothills of central Guanajuato, is thronged with revelers awaiting *el Grito* – the re-enactment of the cry of independence uttered by the rebel priest Miguel Hidalgo on this night in 1810. The cry began Mexico's war of liberation from the Spanish Crown.

It seems appropriate that the struggle for independence began in the geographical heartland of Mexico. Central Mexico is the region most pictured on postcards and in travel magazines. To the outside world, the region's colonial churches, rolling cornfields, picturesque peasants, and traditional fiestas typify Mexico.

Dolores Hidalgo is set in the Bajío ("lowlands"), a fertile swathe cutting across the states of Querétaro, Guanajuato, Jalisco, and Michoacán, that has fed the ravenous capital of the country farther south for a millennium. Now, farming in the Bajío is increasingly mechanized, as US and British (Grand Metropolitan) corporations harvest very un-Mexican crops like broccoli and Brussels sprouts for export. The central–northern Pacific-coast state of Sinaloa has long been a key supplier of winter vegetables, notably tomatoes, to the United States.

Regional rivalries in central Mexico are strong. Jalisco, with its flower-filled capital of Guadalajara, the nation's second largest city (5 million), dominates the west. A conservative Catholic bastion, paradoxically famed for its mariachi music and beautiful women, the city has been beset by intense drug activity in recent years, a suspected factor in the slaying of the Cardinal of Guadalajara in May 1993.

Traditional Catholicism pervades the region and illuminates its history. The Cristiada (1925–29), pitted Catholic zealots against Mexico's revolutionary army in Guanajuato, Jalisco, and Michoacán.

Central Mexico is dotted with patriotic shrines like Dolores

Miguel Hidalgo, as depicted by muralist José Orozco, Government Palace, Guadalajara

(Tony Morrison, South American Pictures)

Hidalgo. Mexico's first constitution (1814) was promulgated in Apatzingán, Michoacán, and the revolutionary 1917 constitution that reigns today was drawn up in the city of Querétaro.

The provincial cities of central Mexico contain some of the fastest growing urban populations in the country. Shrinking plot sizes and the decapitalization of the agricultural sector have forced many to abandon their farms and *ejidos* (land held in common distributed under the land reform program). Michoacán and Jalisco in the west and Zacatecas to the east are traditional feeder states, sending their young men – and, increasingly, their young women – as migrants to the US. Whole communities of émigrés from these states have been created in California and Texas. Gómez Farias, a small eastern Michoacán town, has sent undocumented workers to the northern California agricultural center of Watsonville for over a century, according to investigations carried out at the Colegio de Michoacán.

Economically and politically, central Mexico is tied tightly to the capital, which is high above in the volcano-studded high plateau of the *altiplano*, from which power has historically radiated. Under the snow-capped peaks of Popocatépetl, straddling the states of Mexico and Puebla, ancient civilizations flourished. At the far northeastern end of the valley, the Toltecs ruled what is now Tula, Hidalgo, and the great pyramids of Teotihuacán in Mexico state were power centers at the time of Christ. The Aztec empire flourished at Tenochtitlán in the midst of the lake-covered valley, on an island that is now called Mexico City.

Mexico's South

The 1994 uprising of the rebel Zapatista Army of National Liberation in Chiapas near the Guatemalan border focused fresh attention on Mexico's resource-rich but impoverished south. In several key respects, the rebels were emblematic of the region: they were mostly Mayan Indians whose ancestors ruled the still highly indigenous southeast and they took the name of Emiliano Zapata, "The Liberator of the South," a national icon recognized as the most incorruptible leader of the Mexican Revolution.

From 1910 to 1919, Zapata rode through the states of Morelos, Guerrero, and Puebla, south of Mexico City, fighting to recover the land of Nahua villagers from the creole *hacienda* (estate) owners. Rebellion is still endemic in this Nahuatl-speaking triad.

Descending from the fertile volcanic plateau of Morelos, Guerrero is bordered by the western Sierra Madre. As in much of the south, class contrasts in Guerrero are as startling as the topography: the pricey resort of Acapulco shares the same state as La Montana, demographically the poorest indigenous area in the nation.

Tourists in Acapulco   *(Tony Morrison,*
                                         South American Pictures)

Next door, Oaxaca is an equally mountainous – and even more Indian – state. Nine distinct ethnic groupings, enclosed by jagged sierras, range from the Mixtecs or "Cloud People" clustered around Huahuapan de León, to, on the isthmus at Tehuantepec and Juchitán, the coastal Zapotecs, a unique matriarchal culture in which women are the vanguard of commercial and social activity.

Like Guerrero, the Oaxaca coastline is lined with luxury resorts: Puerto Escondido, a popular spa, is on the southern fringe of Mexico's Afro zone, which is inhabited by the descendants of slaves who settled along this remote coast in the 18th century.

The overland bridge from the Pacific to the Caribbean begins on the isthmus at the west coast oil port of Salina Cruz – it is only 150 miles east by rail (and pipeline) across the narrow neck of Mexico to Veracruz, a state whose long, curving expanse accounts for a quarter of the nation's Caribbean coastline. Often misrepresented as a tranquil tropical paradise, Veracruz is a complex combination of cultures and geography. Nahua-descended Indians are pushed into the rugged sierras while cattle-ranching *caciques* (rural bosses) dominate the rich coastal foothills. Petroleum production thrives at Poza Rica in the north, not far from the important ruins around Tajín, and Coatzacoalcos on the Tabasco-Chiapas border is the nation's petrochemical center.

Oil wells stud southern horizons, fuelling domestic industry and earning a large chunk of Mexico's export income. More than a hundred platforms bob offshore in the Caribbean near Ciudad del Carmen, on the Yucatán peninsula. Leaky oil pipelines snake in and out of Coatzacoalcos, poisoning the river and befouling the air (the city is the most environmentally damaged in Mexico). In the Tabasco swamps and the heart of the Lacandón jungle, Pemex, the national oil company, drills numerous wells.

Tabasco and Chiapas are resource powerhouses. In addition to petroleum production, Tabasco is a major supplier of fruit, fish, and meat to national and international markets. But little of the exported wealth is returned to the region. Chiapas generates nearly half of Mexico's hydroelectric power, yet two thirds of the homes of the indigenous peoples of this huge state do not have electricity. One out of every three *Chiapanecos* is a Mayan Indian.

Mayan culture permeates the southeast. Tourists trek the "Route of the Maya" from the palaces of Palenque on the Chiapas–Tabasco border northeast to Uxmal and Chichén-Itzá, outside Mérida, near the tip of the broad limestone tongue of the Yucatán peninsula. In the southeast, the Mayan language lives on in the Tzotzil speakers in the Altos of Chiapas, through the Chontal lowlands of Tabasco, out to the Yucatán where Mayan remains the *lingua franca.*

On the Yucatán peninsula, the Mayan motif is ubiquitous. Even hotels in the posh tourist resort of Cancún in Quintana Roo are shaped like Mayan pyramids. Ironically, both were built by the same people – the hotels constructed by Mayan day laborers from the region's impoverished rural townships.

The Capital

Promptly at six each afternoon, a trumpet blares and soldiers goose-step out of the National Palace to lower the great green, white, and red flag that flies high over the Plaza of the Constitution or *zócalo* in the historic center of Mexico City. This nightly ceremony, unfailingly witnessed by hundreds of patriotic citizens, is symbolic of the *zócalo's* place at the center of power and change in Mexico. What happens in this plaza, and the city that surrounds it, has always determined the fortunes of Mexico.

Just as the *zócalo* lies at the heart of this high mountain (7,400 feet) capital, the capital is at the core of the nation's economic and political life. Over a quarter of the nation's economic output is produced here, with half of the nation's industrial plants and a fifth of its electorate in residence. Power continues to radiate from Mexico City just as it did in pre-Conquest times. Despite the devastating 1985 earthquake, after which bureaucratic decentralization was decreed, every government ministry continues to be headquartered in the capital as is the Federal Congress. All decisions of national importance are made in Mexico City. Culture, as well as political and economic direction, is framed in the capital at the rococo Fine Arts Institute and the monumental National Anthropological Museum in

Chapultepec Park, not far from Los Pinos, the presidential palace.

What the world knows as Mexico City is a 980-square-mile enclave, divided into sixteen delegations or boroughs, and designated as the Federal District on Mexico's administrative map. To complicate matters, the bulk of the city's 20 million inhabitants, the largest conurbation on the planet, actually lives in what is termed the "urban stain," encompassing a dozen surrounding cities in Mexico state. Such impoverished lake-bed municipalities as Nezahualcoyotl and Chalco (both with multi-million populations) form a "misery belt" from which millions of minimum wage workers commute each day into downtown Mexico City.

Worse, the city proper and its vast suburban areas are a confusing patchwork of overlapping jurisdictions, often governed by rival political parties, making it difficult to coordinate policies – in such crucial areas as water supplies, transportation, and air quality – that would benefit the entire greater metropolitan area.

Until recently, the metropolitan area's population was growing by seven percent a year, swelled by the influx of poor, rural peasants to the city. But that growth has slowed as companies and middle-class residents have relocated to medium-sized towns and suburban bedroom communities, like Santa Fe and Querétaro, both to the northwest of Mexico City.

The government's failure to encourage investment in agriculture has increased urban and US-bound migration from generation to generation. Today the capital, like all Mexican cities, is hemmed in on all sides by *colonias* (neighborhoods) of new arrivals, mostly from the rural south.

Mexico City residents fill up from a water tanker during a water shortage

(L. Addario/ Network Photographers)

Air pollution in downtown Mexico City. *(Tony Morrison/ South American Pictures)*

Unscrupulous speculators sell off lots, and shacks are thrown up on bare hillsides. *Colonos* then lobby the authorities to legalize their presence and provide services such as electricity and drainage.

The swelling populace makes Mexico City hungry for the nation's resources – the capital consumes 40 percent of the nation's meat supply. Trucks pour into the megalopolis laden with produce and grain from the south and center of the country. Distribution is organized from the enormous *Centro de Abastos* (supply center) and retailed at the ancient La Merced market complex near the historic center. The upmarket Lomas de Chapultepec neighborhood eats more meat each year than the entire state of Oaxaca.

If feeding so many millions is a concern, quenching their thirst is a nightmare. Mexico City consumes 60 cubic meters of water every second of the day – ground water sources 100 miles away in Mexico state are running dry. The megalopolis generates 11,000 tons of solid waste daily and 2.6 million homes (17 percent) have no drainage. Twenty thousand tons of fecal dust circulate in the spring winds and the acid rain that falls in the summer dumps heavy metals upon the *chilangos* (as residents of Mexico City are known).

In 1958, the novelist Carlos Fuentes published a visionary novel about life in Mexico City entitled *Where the Air is Clear*. By the mid-1990s, Mexico City's air quality was the worst in the world, with winter-time thermal inversions producing such high ozone levels that migrating

Canadian starlings plummeted dead from the sky. In November 1996, a five-day smog emergency sent 400,000 people to hospitals and contributed to the deaths of 300 people.

Since then, the introduction of unleaded gasoline, enforcement of stringent emission rules for cars (particularly the requirement of catalytic converters for all new vehicles) and the gradual re-location of industry away from the city limits has greatly improved the city's air quality. Whereas in 1995 pollution exceeded unacceptable levels 9 days out of 10, six years later smog alerts were becoming a rare event, with falling levels of sulfur dioxide, nitrogen dioxide, carbon monoxide, lead, and particulates.

Despite the difficulties and dangers of urban life, gridlocked traffic (5 million cars circulate every day), polluted air, and a police force that assaults and extorts with numbing regularity, *chilangos* enjoy one of the liveliest metropolises in the Americas, where political and cultural ferment seems always to be brewing fresh surprises. From the bohemian enclaves of Condesa and Roma, to the exquisite colonial neighborhoods of Coyoacán and San Angel, to the breathtaking beauty of the *centro histórico* (historical center), Mexico City is simply one of the most exciting urban centers in the region.

Although Mexico City is forever tearing down and rebuilding its skyline, an abundant supply of history keeps the past always at one's fingertips – sometimes just beneath the surface of contemporary streets. The *Templo Mayor* (Great Temple) next to Mexico City's vast zócalo was unearthed in 1978 by utility workers laying down electrical lines, while the never-ending digging of the capital's subway system yields a rich harvest of sacrificial stones and shrines to Aztec deities.

While finance ministry technocrats chat up global trading partners from their National Palace offices, Aztec dancers pound the *zócalo* down below and *ambulantes* (street vendors) hawk *alegría*, or amaranth seed cakes, as they have in this same spot for the past thousand years.

2.   PEOPLE AND THEIR HISTORY

¡Viva México!

Hidalgo's time-honored shout "*¡Viva México!*" ("Long Live Mexico!") which now tops off all patriotic fiestas, political speeches, and even anti-government protests, raises a pointed question: why do so many distinct peoples, rooted in such sharply regionalized geographies, express allegiance to one country called Mexico?

The unifying concept of *Mexicanidad* (Mexican-ness) assumes a common heritage of ancient indigenous civilizations, European cultural impositions, indignation at repeated invasion from the north and the legacy of a revolution that killed a million Mexicans. Mexican history is open to many interpretations, but it is a shared event.

Despite the obvious risks of generalization, the Mexican character is shaped by the strength of an extended family unit that includes *padrinos* (godfathers) and *compadres* (loyal friends). One's loyalties are first to family, then to the land and region of one's birth (*patria chica*), and then to the country at large (*patria grande*).

The family is like a miniature state-within-a-state, in which the individual is expected to subordinate his or her needs to the collective, in the interest of the greater good. In return, the extended family protects and takes care of its own – providing financial, material, and moral support. The Mexican family is a nurturing but also an authoritarian entity; it discourages independence, and frowns on individualistic behavior. Mexicans tend to live with their parents until they are married, sometimes well into their 20s and 30s.

Mexicans adore their over-protective mothers, who often raise their children with little help from absentee fathers. They also feel strongly about religion – they are often devout Catholics or fiercely anti-Catholic – though Mexicans as a whole have secular views when it comes to education, contraception, divorce, and abortion (which is illegal in Mexico).

Homosexuality is taboo, and gay-bashing is common. According to the non-governmental Citizens Commission against Homophobic Hate Crimes, an average of three Mexicans die in anti-gay violence every month. Often, gay adolescents are killed by their own parents out of shame. Only in bohemian enclaves, like Colonia Condesa in Mexico City, is homosexuality openly tolerated. Mexico City is the only jurisdiction in the country to have passed an ordinance prohibiting discrimination based on sexual orientation, but it is rarely enforced.

Mexican men and women both struggle with machismo. But it is women who bear the brunt of society's often contradictory attitudes over the appropriate role they should play in an increasingly urban, modernizing nation. Women play a growing role in the urban workforce, especially among professionals; almost half of university students are now female. But they also feel intense pressure to embrace traditional roles as mothers and housewives, and they may be stigmatized and ostracized by their families if they show too much independence.

Many Mexican men seem genuinely ambivalent about this state of affairs. They feel threatened by these more assertive, more demanding, and more independent women; at the same time they are also attracted to these free spirits, who seem to have thrown off the bonds of tradition and religion. But professional, educated Mexican women often find it difficult to find romantic partners. Increasingly, they lead solitary lives as single women, or turn to a relatively new phenomenon in Mexico – dating agencies – to find a mate.

Aguantar (to endure) is an important verb in the Mexican lexicon, best defined as exhibiting a stoic if disdainful patience in the face of the corruption and injustices that pervade the political system. "The Mexican face is a mask – even his smile," wrote Octavio Paz in his insightful, Nobel-prize winning essay on *Mexicanidad, The Labyrinth of Solitude* (1950). Mexicans display a mordant fatalism that personifies Death as a dancing skeleton (*La Calavera*). Like the image of the Virgin of Guadalupe, the *calaca* or *calavera* is a potent icon of *Mexicanidad*.

Another powerful symbol is *La Malinche*, the Chontal noblewoman who became the companion of the Spanish conqueror Hernán Cortés. The children of Cortés and "Doña Marina" were the first *mestizos*, some would say the first Mexicans. La Malinche is both loved and loathed. She betrayed her people by consorting with a foreigner, yet she was the mother of *la raza*, the "cosmic race," her children the golden fruit of two inspired cultures. La Malinche remains a symbol of submission to foreign domination, first by the *gachupines* ("spur-wearers," or Spanish) and then by the *gringos* (the word is said to be derived from the green uniforms worn by US Marines during the 1848 invasion). The Mexicans' sense of themselves as one people is founded upon the extremely durable bedrock of ancient roots and common tribulations.

The concept of *Mexicanidad* has long been fashionable among left-wing intellectuals, who define it as an embracing of folk and indigenous traditions and a rejection of American culture. There is still a strong anti-American current among student radicals – especially the militants responsible for the 1999 strike at the National Autonomous University of Mexico (UNAM), whose distrust of American influence is coupled with loathing for the perceived ill-effects of globalization.

But anti-gringo sentiment was never very widespread among the Mexican public at large. Moreover, a younger generation of writers, artists, and intellectuals today are far more at ease with the cultural influence of the neighbor to the north. Whereas an older generation of Mexican opinion-makers were brought up on European intellectual traditions – and often did graduate studies in Spain or France – younger ones tend to have studied in the United States or Canada.

Class is also an important dividing line in today's Mexico. Although the vast majority of Mexicans are of mixed European and indigenous descent, a current of racial discrimination runs through Mexican society. Darker complexions are synonymous with *la clase popular* (working class); fair complexions with the middle- and upper-classes. The faces on Mexican television are so overwhelmingly fair-skinned, blond-haired, and blue-eyed that one might think it was Swedish TV. Even supposedly indigenous characters on TV are played by white actors.

Educated Mexicans scorn their working-class counterparts as *nacos* (plebian), while the latter deride the pretentious and mannered upper-class person as *fresa* (literally, "strawberry"). Social mobility is almost non-existent in a country where public education and job growth are inadequate to the needs of a swelling population of largely urban poor, who were once memorably described by the late TV magnate Emilio Azcárraga as *los jodidos* ("those who are screwed").

Indigenous Mexico

The 500th anniversary of the European invasion was marked by mobilizations all over Mexico. Up in the capital, it took two hours for all the contingents to march into the *zócalo*. The final group to arrive were Nahuas from Veracruz's Zongolica Sierra and the banner they carried read: "They pulled down our forests, cut off our branches, burned our trunks – but they could not kill our roots."

Unlike Peru, Bolivia, and Guatemala, where indigenous peoples are in the majority, in Mexico most of the native population was assimilated in a *mestizo* culture. It's estimated that some 90 percent of Mexicans are of mixed European and indigenous ancestry. In effect, most Mexicans are descended from both conquerors and conquered – a virtually unique situation in the Americas.

The quantification of Mexico's remaining pure-blooded indigenous population is a subject of debate. The 2000 census found that 7.3 million people spoke an indigenous language, although 2 million of those denied being Indian – apparently because of the social stigma attached to the term. Another 1 million people who didn't speak any native language claimed to be indigenous. The governmental National Indigenous Institute (INI), using a different methodology, estimates the Amerindian population at 10.6 million.

Estimates of the indigenous population of Mexico at the time of the Conquest fall between 12 and 25 million, but a century after Cortés first touched shore, only 1.2 million remained, a loss at least equal to two European holocausts. Although Spanish treatment of the Amerindian population was exceptionally brutal, most indigenous deaths were actually from diseases brought by the colonizers – 800,000 dead were counted during a single smallpox epidemic in 1545. By contrast, Mexico's Indian population is growing today at a faster pace than the non-Indian and their numbers are expected to top pre-Conquest levels early in the 21st century.

Fifty-six distinct *pueblos indios* (Indian peoples) live in Mexico. Thirteen states, seven of them in the south, are regarded as "eminently indigenous" by the INI. Nahuatl speakers are the most numerous, with 1.4 million. Concentrated in central Mexico, the Nahuas are the direct descendants of the Aztecs and other Mexica (Valley of Mexico) cultures. 665,000 Mayan speakers are spread through the southeast and 425,000 Zapotecs inhabit the Isthmus and sierras of Oaxaca. Other numerically and culturally significant groups, ranging from tens to hundreds of thousands, include the Purépechas (Michoacán), the Huicholes and Coras (Jalisco-Nayarit), the Tarahumaras (or Raramuri) of Chihuahua, and the Yaquis and Mayos of the Sonora desert. At the bottom end of the numbers pile are fourteen pueblos with less than a thousand surviving members.

Despite geographical and linguistic disparities, the conditions of life for Mexico's indígenas are universally difficult. Most of the 18 million "extreme poor," as defined by the United Nations, are concentrated in the 803 predominantly Indian municipalities on Mexico's political map. Indian life expectancy, infant and maternal survival rates, literacy and income levels, are all well below that of non-Indians. Emigration flows from Indian villages are some of the highest in the nation – entire villages in the Mixtec Sierra are abandoned by all except the very old and the very young.

Diego Rivera's larger-than-life murals depict the martyrdom of the Aztec emperors. Schoolbooks and breweries honor the nation's Indians on their covers and beer bottle labels. Nonetheless, racism and paternalism are institutional in Mexican society and the only social contacts the privileged classes have with native peoples are with maids and shoeshine-boys. Until quite recently, Mayan Indians in San Cristóbal de las Casas in the Chiapas highlands deferentially stepped off the sidewalk to allow white and *mestizo* burghers to pass. Indians who managed to get into university and train as professionals were tacitly encouraged to assimilate into mainstream society, and most did so.

Despite its stoic countenance, *México indígena* is acquiescing less and less with traditional discrimination. Because most Indians are also subsistence farmers (*campesinos*), they have long been in the forefront of the struggle for agrarian justice – Emiliano Zapata was a Nahuatl speaker. Rejecting the paternalism of the National Indigenous Institute, whose policy of *indigenismo* has historically been directed more toward preserving folk art than improving the daily living conditions of Mexico's Indians, *México indígena* has organized itself to resist racism and government inaction through Councils of Elders, artisan collectives, regional and national alliances, and even by armed rebellion. Amerindian intellectuals are increasingly finding ways to assert on their identity, through professional groups – like the Association of Indigenous Lawyers – and a growing native-language mass media that includes radio stations.

The 1994 Zapatista uprising by four Chiapas Mayan groups resonated powerfully among the nation's indigenous cultures. Today, the *pueblos indios* are demanding administration of their own autonomous regions. The southern state of Oaxaca, with one of Mexico's largest concentrations of native people, is on the forefront. In 1998, it adopted the country's most progressive indigenous rights bill, granting sweeping cultural and political autonomy. Some 412 native towns there have chosen traditional forms of self-government, levying taxes in the form of *tequio* (voluntary labor).

A similar federal law was passed by the Mexican Congress in April 2001, in response to the long-simmering Zapatista rebellion. A native Otomi, Xochitl Galvez, is the government's first-ever Indian affairs adviser with cabinet rank, and there are plans to help indigenous people exploit their own strengths in traditional medicine, organic farming, and other fields to escape poverty. "The oldest peoples are now the vanguard," writes agrarian historian Antonio García de León.

From the Ruins

Mexico's indigenous civilizations are rooted in water and corn. Hunter-gatherers from the north swept into the Valley of Mexico 15,000 years ago but the domestication of corn – first harvested as a wild grass – is not recorded until 4000 BC, south of the valley, at Tehuacán, Puebla.

The Olmec civilization, centered at the curve of the Caribbean coast in Tabasco and Veracruz, is called the "Mother Culture' in Mexican schoolbooks, but the mother is long gone. The Olmecs, who flourished between 1200 and 800 BC, left few clues about themselves other than the enigmatic stone heads with distinctly negroid features that are clustered around La Venta, Tabasco. Olmec fragments have been unearthed as far away as Guerrero on the Pacific Coast, indicating the reach of this first Mexican corn culture.

Maize cultivation in the Valley of Mexico took hold around 3000 BC but did not become dominant until the first millennium before Christ when underground springs at Teotihuacán, 25 miles north of what is now Mexico City, attracted hill dwellers to settle the plain. By the first century BC, Teotihuacán had become the first New World city, with 20,000 permanent residents. The Pyramid of the Sun at its center has a base that equals that of Cheops, the great pyramid at Giza, Egypt, one of the Seven Wonders of the World.

Teotihuacán's population grew alarmingly (200,000 by the fifth century AD) and, unable to support so many people, the city entered into decline. A prolonged drought during the second half of the first millennium AD made the once mighty city-state easy pickings for Chichimeca nomads from the north.

The fall of Teotihuacán around AD 750 roughly parallels the collapse of other dominant cultures. Founded circa 500 BC just outside of what is now the capital of Oaxaca, Monte Albán, a civilization represented today by the Zapotecs, is believed to have fallen victim to the same deadly syndrome of population growth and ecological imbalance.

Similarly, the Mayan city-states of Palenque (Chiapas), Tikal (Guatemala), and Copán (Honduras) were abandoned during this period. The Mayans, whose apogee came between AD 200 and AD 900 (although they date their calendar from 3114 BC), created complex cities and advanced hieroglyphics, studied astronomy and the laws of time, and developed sophisticated mathematics that appreciated the quantity of zero – all while Europe was still languishing in the Dark Ages. But despite the brilliance of their thinkers, the Mayans did not understand the delicate jungle eco-system upon which they depended. The devastation of their forests, combined with a drought that extended throughout Meso-America, strained the carrying capacity of the land and made sustaining the cities impossible.

There were no immediate successors in central Mexico. Chichimeca tribes swept south from the arid deserts and mountains and settled Tlaxcala, Cholula, and the Valley of Mexico. Around AD 1050, a Chichimeca-based culture at Tula came into ascendancy. The Toltecs ("builders" in contemporary Nahuatl) constructed a white city resplendent with temples to Quetzalcoatl, the Plumed Serpent, borrowed from the Teotihuacán pantheon. As with its predecessor corn cultures, Toltec civilization succumbed to drought in the mid-13th century. Legend has Quetzalcoatl abandoning his people because of their sins but promising to come again from the land of the dawn, to the east. Today, the Otomíes (Nahnus) claim descendency from the Toltecs.

Carrying the image of their butterfly warrior god Huitzilopochtli, the Aztecs were the last of the Chichimeca nomads to arrive in the Valley of

The first meeting between Moctezuma and Cortéz.

Mexico. Huitzilopochtli ordained that a city be founded where an eagle was seen devouring a snake and just such a location was sighted on an island in Lake Texcoco – the founding of Tenochtitlán (at what is now Mexico City's Santo Domingo Plaza) in 1325 is commemorated on the Mexican flag.

Despite their scruffy beginnings on a similar island (Aztlán in the territory of Nayarit), and their belligerent demeanor, honed by centuries of nomadic rapine, the Aztecs claimed descendence from the now-exalted Toltecs. Entering into shifting alliances with other powers around the lake, the Aztecs achieved supremacy in the Valley of Mexico by 1427.

The Aztec-Mexicas sought agrarian self-sufficiency not susceptible to the droughts that had cut short those who came before them. The *chinampa* system of agriculture, using floating islands (still cultivated in the Xochimilco district), produced sufficient corn, chili peppers, and calabash to feed the growing city, which by 1480 contained 70,000 residents, an extensive canal system, and increasingly blood-smeared sacrificial altars.

The Aztec empire was built on military might and the subjugation of vassal states by a warrior class. Wars were fought not so much to vanquish the enemy on the battlefield but to capture candidates for sacrifice to the deities that kept the Aztec universe in balance. Tenochtitlán, like all of

Mexico's ancient cultures, was controlled by a theocracy that demanded increased blood sacrifice as much to feed its own ambitions as to ensure sufficient rain and bountiful corn harvest.

The decline of Aztec supremacy is often dated from the death of Tlacaelel (1496), the tlatoani or "kingmaker" who had been the power behind the throne for seven decades. Bereft of his guidance, the ninth Aztec emperor, Moctezuma II, arrogantly declared himself a god and dispatched vast armies 600 miles south to subdue unruly vassals on the fringe of the empire. Demands for tributes of sacrificial victims spurred increasing discordance and rebellion in the provinces.

Meanwhile, Tenochtitlán, now swollen to 200,000 inhabitants, was, like its modern counterpart of Mexico City, becoming increasingly unmanageable. Floods washed over the city and comets were seen streaking the night sky. Moctezuma, a superstitious ruler, is said to have panicked when he heard that a great vessel with billowing wings had been sighted off the Yucatán. The Emperor was convinced that Quetzalcoatl had come again.

Conquest and Colony

The Spanish ships touched shore at the Yucatán and Tabasco in 1517 and 1518. Thirty-three-year-old Hernán Cortés, a soldier of fortune from dirt-poor Extremadura, captained the third expedition, which he himself financed. After tracing the path of his predecessors, Cortés boldly veered northwest, sweeping up the Veracruz coast, and dropped anchor on Good Thursday, 20 April 1519, not far from Laguna Verde, where Mexico's only nuclear reactor is now located. Moctezuma, convinced that Quetzalcoatl had returned, sent emissaries bearing gifts of gold, which only whetted the greed of the Europeans.

The Aztecs were over-extended and their dominion riddled with revolt. First the Totonacos and then the Tlaxcaltecos aligned with Cortés to throw off Tenochtitlán's yoke. Four hundred Spanish soldiers marched into the uplands with horses, cannons, and 20,000 Indian recruits. First they defeated the Cholulans, then climbing between the snowcapped Popocatépetl and Iztaccihuatl volcanoes at the "Paso de Cortés," they attacked the Valley of Mexico.

Moctezuma now saw that the fall of Tenochtitlán was inevitable. On November 8, just seven months after landing on Mexican soil, Cortés marched unimpeded across the causeway into the Aztec island-stronghold. The city itself was bigger than any he had ever seen in Spain.

Moctezuma quickly pledged submission to the Crown and, strenuously prodded by Cortés, forsook human sacrifice and embraced the Catholic faith. But members of the Aztec imperial court were not so easily persuaded. As resistance brewed, the Spanish took Moctezuma hostage and eventually murdered him. The emperor was replaced, first by Cuitlahuac, and then by Cuauhtémoc, the young "descending eagle." Cortés and his troops were obliged to withdraw twice from Tenochtitlán only to return, in the spring of 1521, with boats fashioned in Tlaxcala to speed his forces across the lake. The siege of the city lasted 75 days and Tenochtitlán finally fell on August 21 when Cortés captured Cuauhtémoc. Today the site is immortalized by a fading plaque posted above a used auto parts store on Constancia Street in the inner-city Peralvillo neighborhood. The Fifth Sun, which defined the limits of Aztec rule, had been extinguished. "And so the Mexicans came to their end," the Tlaxcaltecos inscribed in their codices.

The consolidation of conquest was carried out by the cannon and the whip, the Cross, and, most of all, the plague. Only a third of Tenochtitlán's inhabitants survived the first year. In the first 100 years of the colony, the indigenous population of New Spain (which then stretched from north of Chiapas up to the borders of what is today Louisiana) was reduced to a tenth of its former size. Smallpox, pneumonia, even measles and mumps killed millions. In turn, the Indians introduced the Spanish to a disease of their own – syphilis.

Famine accompanied the plagues. The environmental balance developed by the Aztecs collapsed. Hillsides were denuded to rebuild and fuel the capital, and the soil washed down to clog up the lakes with silt. Cattle herds roamed the countryside, devastating Indian lands that had been ceded to the Conquistadores as huge *encomiendas*. The surviving Indians were first enslaved, then freed in 1540 through the insistence of Catholic bishops. Africans were imported to fill the vacuum. By 1650, 20 percent of the population of New Spain – 160,000 people – was of African descent.

The 1545 discovery of rich silver veins 200 miles north of Mexico City in Zacatecas proved a bonanza for the Habsburg dynasty. For the next 100 years (until Peruvian production surged to the forefront), New Spain's silver was the currency of the world.

The 1600s are labeled "the forgotten century" of Mexican history, but during this period several institutions were created that still survive today. Haciendas replaced the *encomiendas* as the focus of rural life, bringing sometimes brutal order to agricultural production. The great colonial cities such as Morelia (then Valladolid), Puebla, and Zacatecas were built. Because Spain allowed no manufacturing in its colonies, *obrajes* (workhouses) were clandestinely opened and Puebla prospered through their production of cloth and pottery. The Church enforced mass conversions via the Inquisition (the gruesome executions of heretics held in the zócalo were the most spectacular outside of Spain itself).

Another instrument for spreading the One True Faith was the dark-

The Virgin of Guadalupe.　　　*(Paul Smith)*

skinned Virgin of Guadalupe, said to have revealed herself to the Indian Juan Diego in 1531 on Tepeyac hill to the north of Mexico City, the site of a temple dedicated to Tonantzin, the Aztec earth mother. Such syncretic substitutions were commonplace – cathedrals were erected atop temples whose stones were still stained with the blood of sacrificial victims. The old gods were still venerated under the names of the new saints, in languages and rituals that live into the present.

The cult of the Virgin of Guadalupe did not achieve popularity until the 17th century when the creole class – the mixed-blood, light-skinned descendants of Spanish and Indians – took up her banner. Although New Spain was racially diverse, color bars were impenetrable – sixteen separate castes, distinguished by skin color gradations, were devised to prevent social mixing. Indians, Blacks, and mestizos occupied the lowest rungs while the few pure-bred Spaniards – the white *gachupines* – ruled the roost. A notch below, the creoles, who considered themselves *Americanos* because of their New World birth, fumed at the limits of their social status.

The defeat of the Spanish Armada in 1588, the devastating 30-Year War, and the degeneracy of the Habsburg succession left the mother country a shell of what it had been at the time of the Conquest. New Spain, meanwhile, was in its ascendancy. Trade with both East and West boomed independently of the Crown. From 1565 until the early 19th century, the Manila galleons of the *Nao* fleet brought the riches of the Orient to Acapulco, a west coast port built by the Spanish in their unflinching belief that sailing ever westward would eventually bring them to the east. Goods bound for Spain embarked from Veracruz and took less time to make Sevilla than it took for Zacatecas silver to reach Mexico's east coast.

During the 18th century, New Spain doubled its size to 1.6 million square miles, claiming Texas, California, and what is now the western United States – a land area greater than even Brazil. Between 1742 and 1819, the population doubled to 6.1 million and Mexico City, with 130,000 residents, became the largest in the Americas.

As the 19th century dawned, power and wealth in New Spain was concentrated in a merchant class that included no more than 20,000 native Spanish and 10,000 creoles. They built the colonial mansions that still line the streets of the capital's historic center, dined on European and Oriental delicacies, and even rented noble titles from the Bourbon Crown. Meanwhile, 3.6 million indigenous people and another 2.5 million mestizos and *mulatos* labored in the mines, *obrajes*, and haciendas, far removed from the money economy. The Bishop of Valladolid summed up the system, explaining "This country is divided between those who have nothing and those who have everything."

Liberators, Presidents, Emperors, and Dictators

Mexico's struggle for liberation was one of a dozen insurrections against the mother country between 1808 and 1821. Unlike the uprisings farther south, the startling inequities between the top and the bottom in New Spain determined that liberation would be obtained with maximum bloodshed.

The detonating cause was the struggle of the creole Americanos for a greater share of power, a battle infused by the democratic spirit of the French Revolution and the rebellion of the thirteen American colonies against the English throne. When Napoleon invaded Spain in 1808, wall writings in Mexico City announced that the time was ripe for revolution.

But the uprising did not begin in the capital. A creole country priest in the Bajío of Guanajuato, Miguel Hidalgo, sounded the *grito* of independence on 16 September 1810, after fellow conspirators learned they had been betrayed. Hidalgo was not the only cleric to conspire against the Crown – 400 activist priests participated in the liberation struggle.

Ten thousand people, mostly Indians, mestizos, and mulatos, marched behind Hidalgo and the banner of the Virgin of Guadalupe when the liberating army sacked the state capital. Their fury at the light-skinned overclass was made manifest when they massacred 300 royalists who had sought refuge in the Guanajuato grain storehouse, the Alhóndiga. In Mexico City, the creoles and *gachupines* grew fearful and dispatched the royal army, only 23,000 strong and with few native-born Spanish soldiers in its ranks, to meet Hidalgo. Although the priest's forces by now totaled 100,000, they were badly outgunned. Hidalgo fled north but was captured in Chihuahua and shot. His uprising had lasted just seven months.

José María Morelos y Pavón, a swarthy priest from the hot lands of Michoacán, took up Hidalgo's mantle. Rather than rebuilding the mass army of his predecessor, Morelos dedicated his troops to guerrilla warfare and enjoyed success in the southern provinces until captured and executed while trying to cut the Veracruz road in 1815. His successor, Vicente Guerrero, continued the guerrilla attacks in the west.

Contemporary depiction of Mexican independence wars.

Ironically, liberation finally came from the royal army itself. Augustín de Iturbide, the creole general who had defeated Hidalgo in 1810, forged an alliance with Guerrero and promulgated the "Plan of Iguala," calling for independence from Spain, universal Catholicism, and the union of native-born Mexicans and Spanish to found the new nation. On 27 September 1821, Iturbide rode unimpeded into the capital and Independence was formally declared. Eleven years of insurgency had elapsed since Hidalgo's cry and 600,000 had died, most of them the Indian and mestizo poor. Three hundred years almost to the day since Cortés had taken Tenochtitlán, the Mexicans were free, but it was a freedom enjoyed only by the very few.

The dream of a democratic republic soured quickly. Within months, Iturbide had declared himself emperor and two years later he was publicly executed. Between 1821 and 1855, Mexico had 50 governments, 11 of them under the direction of Antonio Santa Ana. General Santa Ana sacked public treasuries, inexplicably lost major battles, and gave up half of Mexico to the United States, but time and again, desperate legislators invited the romantic, paranoid *Veracruzano* to become president.

Antonio Santa Ana is vilified for having ceded the north of Mexico to the hated gringos. In 1835, the General rushed his troops to Texas, needlessly massacred a garrison of American secessionists at the Alamo, and was routed at the Battle of San Jacinto, setting the stage for US intervention. A decade later, President James Polk annexed Texas under the flag of Manifest Destiny and the Americans crossed the Río Grande, landed marines at Mazatlán on the Pacific Coast and Veracruz on the Gulf. General Winfield Scott followed Cortés' path to Mexico City and by 14 September 1847 the stars and stripes were flying over Chapultepec Castle. The martyred young defenders of that stronghold are honored as *los niños héroes* (the heroic children). The Treaty of Guadalupe Hidalgo, signed on 2 February 1848, handed over 780,000 square miles to Washington – the US western frontier. The discovery of gold in California was kept secret from the Mexican negotiators.

Mexico's modern political history begins with the end of Santa Ana's last presidency in 1855. Liberals, under the leadership of Benito Juárez, seized power and decreed the 1857 Constitution that nationalized Catholic Church property and severely restricted its authority. A conservative backlash, led by Lucas Alamán, plunged the nation into civil war. The Conservatives fought for a centralized, oligarchic system while the long-haired Liberals favored secular federalism.

In 1861, a victorious Juárez reinstated the Constitution and its Laws of Reform, but declared the nation bankrupt and unable to pay its foreign debt. Conservatives dispatched emissaries to Europe, petitioning England, France, and Spain to intervene to save Mexico from the barbarian Liberals and redeem what was owed them. England and Spain sent expeditionary forces but Juárez talked them both into postponing collection. Napoleon III, however, was eager to break US dominance in the Americas. In 1862, as the US Civil War was beginning, the French invaded – the defeat of French troops on May 5 at the Battle of Puebla by Generals Ignacio Zaragoza and Porfirio Díaz and an army of Zacapoaxtla Indians remains a patriotic holiday for Mexicans at home and abroad. But the French regrouped and easily took the capital.

Nostalgic for Old World ways, Conservatives invited Maximilian, a Habsburg archduke of Austria, and his bride, Princess Carlota of Belgium, to become Emperor and Empress of Mexico. The scheme soon backfired as Maximilian, a humanist, embraced the Liberals' program. Meanwhile, the combined French–Conservative armies pushed Juárez's constitutional government north to the Texas border at Paseo del Norte (now Ciudad Juárez). Breaking into guerrilla bands, the president struck back, eventually making movement outside of the capital too dangerous for the emperor's troops. On the southern front, Porfirio Díaz punished the French forces.

By 1865, Napoleon was being pressured by Bismarck's Prussia and needed his army back, while the US Civil War had ended and Washington was threatening to enforce the Monroe Doctrine. Isolated, without army or spirit, his half-mad wife scouring Europe for support, Maximilian was captured and executed on a hill above Querétaro in June 1867. Díaz rode into Mexico City to await Juárez's arrival.

These two powerful *Oaxaqueños* dominated Mexican politics for the next half-century. Juárez was a Zapotec Indian whose ancestors had built Monte Albán. Much like his contemporary, Abraham Lincoln, Juárez was a back-country lawyer determined to defend the underdog. This quest for justice shaped his vision as he climbed the political ladder to become governor of Oaxaca and president of the supreme court. Díaz's climb was equally steep. The son of provincial storekeepers, he rose through the military, known for his endurance and bravery. General Díaz's political vision, however, appears to have been formed mostly by blind ambition. After the French were expelled, Juárez became the first elected president of Mexico ever to complete his term in office. But when Juárez sought to run again in 1871, in defiance of the constitution he had written, which precluded re-election, Díaz rose in Oaxaca. Despite Juárez's death the next year, civil war, and fierce personality politics wracked the nation until 1876 when Díaz declared himself the victor.

Porfirio Díaz reigned so long (34 years) that history has assigned him his own epoch, the *Porfiriato*. The secret of the General's longevity is contained in his slogan, "Order and Progress." Mexico had been at war with itself since 1810 and Díaz enforced a "Pax Porfiriano," using his feared *rurales* (rural police) and *federales* (federal army). Local *caudillos* (strongmen) exercised absolute authority over rebellious Indian and mestizo campesinos and workers. Meanwhile, progress would be assured by foreign investors. The unschooled Díaz surrounded himself with *científicos*, technocrats who believed human perfectibility would be guaranteed by technology. British engineers extended the rail system from 200 to 7,500 miles, opening up the interior of the country to agricultural production for export. Mexican oil found its way onto foreign markets and silver and gold mining was revived under concessions granted to US and European prospectors. Newly electrified industry hummed, but the profits accrued to only a few. Díaz even repaid the foreign debt.

Every four years, the Dictator would run for office in violation of the constitution (sometimes he substituted a crony), winning the presidency eight times and founding Mexico's modern system of electoral fraud.

A hundred years after Independence, on the eve of Díaz's downfall, the vast majority of what now totaled 15 million Mexicans were no better off than when Hidalgo uttered his sacred *grito*. Eighty percent of the population lived in the countryside where landless peasants were bound to the haciendas for life. In the south, Indian peons were press-ganged to cut down the mahogany forests for European consumption. The purchasing power of urban workers was the same as it had been a century before. In 1910, the median life span in Mexico City was only 24 years, versus 45 in Paris. Mexico's long-suffering poor were ripe for another disastrous revolution.

The Mexican Revolution

By the first decade of the 20th century, the geriatric dictatorship could no longer satisfy the needs of the people it governed. Middle-class demands for upward mobility came up against an ageing and impenetrable oligarchy. The militancy of the citizenry was fueled by the writings of the anarchist Flores Magón brothers in their outlawed journal, *Regeneración*. The newly industrialized masses organized into trade unions, but strikes at the Cananea copper mine in Sonora and the textile factories in Río Blanco, Veracruz, were crushed by company thugs and Díaz's *federales*. The peasantry watched as village lands were gobbled up by the haciendas – four times as many rural poor were bound to these estates as lived in the free towns. One Chihuahua estate was as large as Belgium.

The collapse of metal prices in 1907 set off worldwide recession, exacerbating tensions. When, in 1908, Díaz told a US journalist he would not run again two years hence, the door seemed open to change. Five thousand anti-Díaz Liberal Party clubs sprang up throughout Mexico between 1908 and 1910.

Francisco Madero was an unlikely challenger to the dictator. The scion of a wealthy San Luis Potosí family, Madero, a tiny Lenin lookalike with spiritualist pretensions, campaigned up and down the land on the platform of Juárez's 1857 Constitution forbidding re-election. Díaz, infuriated by the upstart's audacity, reversed his decision not to run and clapped his opponent in jail where the challenger and 5,000 supporters spent election day 1910. Stuffing ballot boxes and buying votes, Díaz won re-election handily. The dictator was then 80 years of age.

But Madero was obsessed. Escaping prison, he fled beyond the border to Texas from where he issued a call for the revolution to begin at 6PM on 20 November 1910 in all the plazas of Mexico. The scattered uprisings that followed were concentrated in the north, under the leadership of the rejected candidate for governor of Coahuila, Venustiano Carranza, and two ne'er-do-well cattle thieves from Chihuahua: Francisco Villa and Pascual Orozco. Together with Alvaro Obregón, a Sonora bean farmer, and the dashing peasant leader Emiliano Zapata from Morelos state far to the south, the five later formed the Constitutionalist Army that brought about Díaz's demise. The "Constitutionalists" sought a return to the Constitution of 1857, which barred re-election. Díaz, as commander-in-chief of the government forces, headed the "federal" army.

Using the railroad system, the pride of the *Porfiriato*, to great advantage, Villa's División *del Norte* stormed south from Ciudad Juárez, and, within six months, the decrepit Díaz abdicated, sailing off to France with the dire warning, "The wild beasts have been loosed. Now let us see who can cage them."

Francisco Madero proved a timid liberal who believed in the inviolability of private property and did not grasp the depths of the fury unleashed by his middle-class rebellion. Within days of his 1911 inauguration, Zapata, a one-time ally, rose up in Morelos to take back village lands systematically absorbed by the haciendas. Zapata's "Ayala Plan" was both an agrarian program and a declaration of war against whoever governed in Mexico

City. His crusade did not end until the dashing, mustachioed "Caudillo of the South" was betrayed by Carranza eight years later.

Under fire from the grassroots, with little support from the squabbling Constitutionalists, Madero presented an easy target for an unvanquished Porfirian political class and was soon overthrown by General Victoriano Huerta, who had Madero ignominiously shot outside Mexico City's Lecumberri prison in February 1913. Huerta, who had won his spurs by suppressing Indian rebellions, was warmly praised by the United States for restoring a semblance of law and order.

Huerta's counter-revolution united the bickering Constitutionalists. Militarily, the federal army was weakened by its dependence on unwilling conscripts, and was unable to prevent Obregón's Army of the Northwest from sweeping unimpeded down the Pacific Coast. Huerta's only hope of salvation lay in Washington, but by 1914 Woodrow Wilson was the US president. Huerta did not fit into Wilson's plan to impose his idea of democracy upon Latin America. In one of the more embarrassing moments in the history of US interventionism, Washington landed marines in Veracruz in an effort to block arms shipments to Huerta and nearly succeeded in uniting all warring Mexican factions against the United States. Stripped of US support, the hard-drinking Huerta fled Mexico and died of liver cirrhosis two years later in a Texas jail.

Emiliano Zapata *(Pedro Martinez\South American Pictures)*

Huerta's flight renewed rivalries between the four revolutionary generals. The white-bearded, patrician Carranza was the first to enter the capital and summoned Obregón, Zapata, and Villa to a "sovereign revolutionary convention" to decide who among them should rule. But Zapata and Villa, the most radical of the caudillos, joined forces and appointed their own interim president. Carranza fled eastward to Veracruz, where he was soon joined by Obregón. In December 1914, the peasant armies of Villa and Zapata marched triumphantly into the capital and occupied the National Palace. The meeting of the two revolutionary generals in Xochimilco in the south of the city marked the zenith of the Mexican Revolution.

PROCLAMATION

$5,000⁰⁰ REWARD

FRANCISCO (PANCHO) VILLA

ALSO $1,000. REWARD FOR ARREST OF
CANDELARIO CERVANTES, PABLO LOPEZ,
FRANCISCO BELTRAN, MARTIN LOPEZ

ANY INFORMATION LEADING TO HIS APPREHENSION WILL
BE REWARDED.

CHIEF OF POLICE
Columbus
New Mexico

MARCH 9, 1916

Reward poster for Pancho Villa,
hero of the Mexican Revolution.

*(Pedro Martinez/South
American Pictures)*

Zapata and Villa were both regionalists with no taste for the affairs of state and both soon returned to their home territories, leaving a caretaker president in charge of a defenseless Mexico City. Storming in from the east coast, Obregón forced Villa into two devastating confrontations in Celaya, Guanajuato in April 1915, eliminating half of Villa's troops – all Obregón lost was his right arm. Save for an occasional guerrilla adventure, such as his raid on Columbus, New Mexico in 1916, Villa was never again a factor in the power struggles that consumed the Mexican Revolution.

The neutralization of Villa allowed Carranza to turn his attentions toward Zapata, but the charismatic peasant eluded his pursuers until 10 April 1919 when he was lured to the Chinameca hacienda in southern Morelos on the pretext of obtaining arms and gunned down by federal troops.

Years of unrelenting treachery had left Carranza the unquestioned winner. By 1917, he had consolidated his grip on power and promulgated one of the noblest-sounding constitutions in the world. The new magna carta, still in force today, decreed free public education, workers' rights to strike and to work an eight-hour day. Article 27, which governs agrarian reform, set Zapata's contribution to the revolution in stone, establishing the expropriation and redistribution of hacienda lands to the rural poor. Progressive on paper, the Mexican Constitution was almost immediately violated in practice. By 1924, only 3.5 percent of all hacienda land had been handed out and much of that went to the victorious generals.

Carranza left office reluctantly. Having agreed to turn power over to Obregón in 1920, he tried to move the seat of his government to Veracruz, loading the nation's gold onto his private train, and was shot down by Obregón loyalists.

At least a million Mexicans, perhaps two million, died or fled their country between 1910 and 1920, a toll as great as the fall of Tenochtitlán and the War of Liberation. Famine in 1915 killed tens of thousands, as did the 1917 influenza epidemic. The nation's industrial production was paralyzed and fields were left fallow throughout the land. Once again, the Indian and mestizo poor had paid the highest price, and the dying was not yet over.

Exhausted, the nation mutely obeyed Obregón's dictates as he guided Mexico through three years known as "the Reconstruction." But when the one-armed general sought to turn power over to a fellow Sonoran officer, Plutarco Elías Calles, in 1923, his enemies rose in the north, in a revolt that cost 7,000 more lives.

Plutarco Calles viewed the Catholic Church with disdain, and he closed convents and church-run schools, nationalizing church property and forcing priests and nuns to wear mufti. Cristero guerrillas rose against his revolutionary army in the Bajío between 1926 and 1929. Thirty thousand people are said to have died in the fighting.

But a revolution is what comes after the killing, too. Both Obregón and Calles enlisted artists like Diego Rivera, who were filled with revolutionary fervor and set about monumentalizing the fratricidal bloodshed in the heroic murals that still endure as the image of the Mexican Revolution. Yet, of all the artists the revolution produced, perhaps it was José Guadalupe Posada (d. 1914), the engraver of political cartoons that featured grotesquely grinning *calaveras* (skulls), who best expressed the true nature of the carnage.

Although the echo of the Mexican Revolution was heard throughout the hemisphere and its martyrs have become the martyrs of all the Americas, Mexicans still ponder whether their revolution really was worth the years of desolation the nation was forced to endure.

Death of a Revolutionary, by José Guadalupe Posada.

3. SOCIETY

Institutionalizing the Revolution

Speaking on Mexican television in 1991, Peruvian novelist Mario Vargas Llosa characterized his host's government as "the perfect dictatorship" and the long-ruling Institutional Revolutionary Party (PRI) as "the envy of Latin dictators." The PRI "maintains the appearance of democracy but suppresses it by all means, even the worst, whenever criticism threatens its perpetuation in power." Vargas Llosa was obliged to leave Mexico City the next morning.

The institutionalization of the Mexican Revolution began with Plutarco Elías Calles (1928–33). Faced with the proliferation of more than 300 regional political parties, most headed by local caudillos whose interests were more mercenary than ideological, Calles issued a call for the creation of a national party to prevent further sectarian slaughter. Constituted in 1929 as the Party of the National Revolution, the PRN was more a vehicle for the rule of the "Supreme Chief," as Calles designated himself, than a democratic organization embracing the views of its constituents. Calles imposed his will on the nation by installing three puppet presidents (one was removed by revolt, another resigned).

His final choice, a young revolutionary general and former governor of Michoacán, Lázaro Cárdenas, proved to be Calles' undoing, eventually dispatching the aging strongman into political exile with a copy of *Mein Kampf* under his arm.

Calles created institutions from the rubble of revolution. He established the central bank (the Bank of Mexico) in 1925, the university became autonomous (1929), and Secretary of Education José Vasconcelos set up a public education system. But it is Cárdenas who deserves the credit (and the blame) for transforming the revolution into permanent structures.

An indefatigable traveler in the provinces, willing to listen for hours to the poorest of his constituents, Cárdenas dedicated his presidency to transforming rhetoric into lasting deeds. Although Mexico was wounded by a worldwide depression that cost it two-thirds of its export revenues, Cárdenas shifted resources and priorities toward the underclass with a passion seldom seen in venal Mexican politics. Over 8 million acres of hacienda and government land were distributed to landless peasants, triple the amount of his predecessors. Also rural credit bank and regional and national farmers' organizations were established. Faced with a record-breaking number of strikes, Cárdenas refused to intervene, arguing the workers were only seeking to create a more equitable balance between labor and employers.

In 1938, riding a wave of popular support, General Cárdenas transformed the PRN into the Party of the Mexican Revolution (PRM), incorporating poor farmers (now grouped in the National Campesino Confederation or CNC) and the Mexican Labor Confederation (CTM). Other sectors included "popular organizations," comprising the tiny middle class and government employees, and the military.

Buoyed by his massive popularity, in 1938 Cárdenas also stepped into an oil workers' strike and nationalized a dozen Anglo-American oil companies in an act that instantly converted the General into a Latin American hero. The sense of national pride instilled by the expropriation welded together the nation and the new party, as rich and poor lined up outside the Bellas Artes Institute to donate fine jewelry and the chickens of humble campesinos to a national treasury under siege from an international boycott in retaliation for Cárdenas' bold stroke.

On the international front, President Cárdenas opened Mexico's doors to both Spanish Republicans fleeing Franco's putsch and to European Jews fleeing the Nazis, a policy of political asylum that Mexico honored for decades afterwards. The Colegio de México, today one of the country's most prestigious universities, was founded by exiled Spanish Republicans.

Until the 1990s, Mexico City was a haven for leftists seeking sanctuary from right-wing military dictatorships across the continent – including, at one point, the young Fidel Castro. Mexico was virtually the only government in the hemisphere to maintain friendly relations through the years with Castro's Cuba, despite pressure from the United States. Today, however, with democracies installed throughout Latin America, Mexico more often plays host to students who come to study at its well-respected universities.

Cárdenas' hand-picked successor, General Manuel Avila Camacho, was the most conciliatory member of his cabinet. A wartime president, Avila Camacho enforced a program of national unity that contrasted sharply with Cárdenas' tolerance of social discontent.

United States wartime needs for Mexican natural resources and manpower revived ties with the north that had been rubbed raw by the expropriation of US oil properties. The war also speeded up Mexico's industrialization, as members of "the revolutionary family" – the generals who had emerged victorious from the revolution – became budding industrialists and impresarios.

President Miguel Alemán (1946–52) was the first head of state not to have directly participated in the Revolution. Alemán set about reforming the state party, renaming it the Party of the Institutional Revolution (PRI), and eliminating the military as a sector of the party's corporate structure. Less than a decade after Cárdenas had left office, Alemán directed the state away from serving the needs of the most disadvantaged sectors toward the creation of wealth that one day, he predicted, all Mexicans would share. Although not officially represented in the PRI's corporate structure, the private sector dictated economic policy. Constitutional Article 27 was amended to create loopholes allowing large landowners to rebuild their giant farms. Foreign investors were ardently wooed, as Alemán welcomed Harry Truman, the first US president to set foot in Mexico. Under Alemán and his successors, Adolfo Ruiz Cortines (1952–58), Adolfo López Mateos (1958–64), and Gustavo Díaz Ordaz (1964–70), Mexico enjoyed 6 percent annual growth, but the profits of "the miracle years" ended up in the bank accounts of the few: ten percent of Mexicans held fifty percent of the available wealth.

The PRI: The Limits of Longevity

In its heyday, the Party of the Institutional Revolution (PRI) was often compared with such durable political institutions as the former Soviet Communist Party, Japan's Liberal Democrats, India's Congress Party, or even Chicago Mayor Richard Daley's Democratic machine, dispensing favors to its ward bosses throughout the land and punishing those who refused to play the game.

The president of the country – who was also the effective leader of the PRI – had virtually imperial powers, unchecked in a system where the legislature, the judiciary, and the mass media were subservient to the ruling party. His office would draft laws and constitutional amendments to be rubber-stamped by the PRI-dominated Congress.

The exalted status of the Mexican presidency recalled the figure of the tlatoani – the power behind the Aztec throne. The only constraint on the president's powers was that he was limited to a single six-year term, a *sexenio*, inspired by Madero's rallying cry in his 1910 campaign against Díaz: "Effective Suffrage – No Re-election!"

Outgoing presidents were, however, allowed to select their successors in a secretive ritual known as *dedazo*, (the big finger-point), so that the next head of state could continue his predecessor's policies once in office – though it rarely worked out that way. Indeed, the *dedazo* proved to be increasingly divisive for the party, as in 1987 when a group of prominent dissidents left the PRI over their opposition to the selection of Carlos Salinas de Gortari as its presidential candidate.

At the height of its power, the PRI decided every aspect of life, from how history was recorded to the way the daily news was reported. The party's colors were the colors of the Mexican flag, a proprietary right the opposition repeatedly challenged. Backed by state patronage and absolute control of the electoral machinery, until 1985 the PRI controlled every political office from the federal presidency down to the state and local levels – a phenomenon known as a *carro completo* or "full car." The party's support of thousands of local *caudillos* and *caciques* (strongmen or bosses) guaranteed the PRI a disciplined power base.

But as the 20th century drew to a close, the PRI's hold on power began to unravel. It had come to power in a largely rural, illiterate Mexico receptive to its strident populism and promises of social justice. Its popularity began to wane as the country became predominantly urban and more educated; a mature middle-class emerged that grew impatient with the party's corruption, cronyism, and economic mismanagement; the swelling ranks of young voters became fed up with the lack of opportunities and disgusted with the country's arrogant, out-of-touch leadership; and free market reforms deprived the party of many of the perks and pork-barrel privileges it used to dole out to clients in the PRI-controlled unions and other corporatist groups.

Challenged from without by the surging popularity of the center-right National Action Party in the north and the center-left Party of the Democratic Revolution in the center and south, and from within by factional squabbles – witness the unprecedented 1994 assassinations of both a PRI presidential candidate and the party's secretary general – its share of the presidential vote fell steadily.

The moral corruption of the party was epitomized by Raul Salinas, the elder brother of ex-president Carlos Salinas, who in 1999 was convicted of the murder of his brother-in-law Jose Francisco Ruiz Massieu, the PRI secretary general. Salinas was also found to possess $107 million in a Swiss bank account, accumulated while he was the head of a government agency responsible for food subsidies for the poor. It was confiscated by the Swiss as likely drug proceeds. The tradition of Mexican presidents enriching themselves and their families while in office is long established.

Further scandals rocked the party. A former PRI tourism minister and ex-mayor of Mexico fled the country after being accused of embezzling $43 million. The governor of Yucatán, suspected of collusion with drug traffickers, disappeared as federal police closed in for an arrest. A flawed bailout of the banking system, costing $100 billion (about one-fifth of gross domestic product), vastly enriched PRI supporters in the financial community.

The PRI had to resort to dirty tricks to stay in power in the 1988 presidential elections, when a left-wing ex-PRIsta, Cuauhtemoc Cárdenas – son of the revered ex-president Lázaro Cárdenas – mounted an unexpectedly strong challenge that looked like it might steal victory from the ruling party's candidate, Carlos Salinas. It is widely believed that the PRI fixed the election in favor of Salinas by engineering a mysterious computer shutdown during the vote-count. During the 1997 mid-term elections, the PRI lost control of both the lower house of Congress and the Mexico City government. The very same Cuauhtemoc Cárdenas became Mexico City's first popularly elected mayor.

In the run-up to the 2000 presidential election, the ruling party tried in vain to revamp its image. President Ernesto Zedillo even abandoned the hated *dedazo* in favor of an American-style open primary to choose the party's presidential candidate, in order to head off a potentially crippling internal struggle over the succession – as well as to burnish the PRI's democratic credentials. Interior Secretary Francisco Labastida Ochoa, a gray career bureaucrat backed by the party establishment, emerged victorious from the first-ever PRI primary. He went on to lose decisively to Vicente Fox in the presidential election eight months later.

The American-Style Presidency

Fox inherited a presidency with greatly reduced powers. Unlike his PRI predecessors, his party does not control the Congress. He is scrutinized by a mass media that is independent and scathingly critical – as well as unconstrained by ethical standards and libel laws, which are extremely weak in Mexico.

Hostile PRI-affiliated unions remain the strongest organized labor force in the land, with the ability to mobilize millions of workers, and regard Fox and his promises of free-market reform with suspicion. Even the judiciary, once a compliant tool of past presidents, has shown signs of independent-mindedness in recent years.

Fox won the presidency with 42.7 percent of the vote. But he is more popular than his National Action Party, which is only the second largest party in Congress. The PRI retains the largest number of seats in both houses of the national legislature, obliging the president and his party to co-operate with its old political foes to get laws passed.

The American-style separation of powers codified in the 1917 Constitution, long a charade under the PRI, has become a reality in the federal Congress. Since 1997, the 500-member Chamber of Deputies and the 128-member Senate have gradually acquired real teeth – rejecting or altering bills sent by the president, arguing over the budget, debating issues of national importance. Horse-trading, the art of compromise, the search for consensus – these skills are in their infancy in Mexico's supreme legislative body, but they are taking hold.

A constraint on the presidency is the Constitution, which – unlike its US, Canadian, or British counterpart – is highly detailed, setting out rigid guidelines for everything from social policy to housing, education, religion, energy policy, health, welfare, and a raft of other areas. It is seen as a utopian document with no connection to daily reality as most Mexicans experience it; the fundamental rights and freedoms it sets forth are largely ignored in practice.

The current occupant of *Los Pinos,* the presidential palace, therefore has relatively few levers at his disposal to advance his legislative agenda. But Vicente Fox is the most American-style head of state Mexico has ever had. Like former US president Bill Clinton – to whom he is sometimes compared – his preferred political tactic is to appeal over the heads of Congress directly to Mexican voters, using the office as a bully pulpit to sway public opinion. He realized early on that in an era of democratic politics, the most important battles would be fought in the media.

President Vicente Fox and George Bush

(Corbis)

President Fox is Mexico's most media-savvy politician. A special presidential office does sophisticated public opinion polling on a weekly (even daily) basis, and a former Proctor & Gamble marketing executive hones his image. In contrast to the centralizing, micro-managing instincts of his predecessors, Fox runs the government like the CEO of a large corporation, delegating responsibilities to his cabinet and confining himself to setting broad strategy. But it's unclear whether he can satisfy the enormous expectations he has raised among Mexicans, given the political constraints of Mexico's democratic transition – and his own government's apparent lack of focus. Tellingly, Fox is often compared to Francisco Madero, the well-meaning but ineffectual reformer who led the overthrow of the Porfirio Diaz dictatorship in 1910, but was unable to govern effectively and soon ousted in a coup.

Political Opposition in Mexico

From its inception, the Mexican Revolution produced schisms that opposed the tyranny of the institutionalized revolutionary state. Mexico's Communist Party (founded 1919), along with other Marxist and anarchist tendencies grouped around the *Casa del Obrero Mundial* ("House of the World's Workers") challenged the conservative Calles and his puppet

Zapatistas with flowers in a peace overture
(Chris Sharp/ South American Pictures)

successors. The communists published their combative *Machete* newspaper and attracted militant feminists like Benita Galeana and artists such as Diego Rivera and Tina Modotti.

Although neutralized by Cárdenas' left-leaning policies in the 1930s, the socialist opposition had a firm hold in the labor movement until 1941, when Marxist CTM leader Vicente Lombardo Toledano was replaced by Fidel Velázquez, a former Mexico state milkman. The 1957 railroad strike, and the subsequent mobilizations of teachers and doctors, were led by communists. The Cuban Revolution further fanned resistance to the PRI's "perfect dictatorship" – the events that led to Tlatelolco began with a march on 26 July 1968 to mark the fifteenth anniversary of the beginning of Castro's revolt.

For many Mexicans, the massacre of striking students by the army and police on 2 October 1968 in Mexico City's middle-class Tlatelolco housing complex first exposed the true face of the ruling PRI. Much is still unknown about this watershed moment in contemporary Mexican history: how many victims it produced (337 is the best estimate), where their bodies are buried, who was responsible for giving the orders to fire, and who did the actual shooting. No one has even been held responsible, and the archives on the incident remain closed to scrutiny.

Tlatelolco marked a generation of young Mexicans, beginning a tradition of political protest and militancy that was much in evidence during a more recent event – the 1999 student strike at the National Autonomous

University of Mexican (UNAM), Latin America's largest university. An attempt to raise tuition fees at the public institution led to the occupation of university buildings by a group of radical students and a nearly complete shut-down that lasted 292 days. It was finally broken up peacefully by the police.

By no means has all radical opposition come from the left. The fascist Sinarquista movement in the Bajío was an outgrowth of the *Cristero* rebellion. The Sinarquistas sent their "black shirts" into the streets in support of Hitler's Germany but regrouped, after the war, as the far-right Mexican Democratic Party (PDM), opting for electoral participation rather than confrontation.

Still, the PRI rarely used the blunt weapon of repression against its rivals, preferring subtler methods that became known as "velvet repression." Mexicans like to tell the story of a former president, Luis Echeverría, who while on a visit to the Soviet Union in the early 1970s, compared notes with Leonid Brezhnev on how to run a one-party state. Brezhnev is said to have expressed admiration for the PRI's unique brand of soft authoritarian rule. Echeverría is said to have replied: "The only difference between our two systems is that when you have a problem, you subtract. When we have a problem, we add."

What he meant was that Mexico's ruling elite preferred to buy off its enemies, instead of crushing them as the Soviets did. Critical writers, intellectuals, and artists were offered grants, scholarships to study abroad, artistic commissions, prizes, exhibitions, and publishing contracts – part of a "cultural welfare state" that was the most extensive and generous in Latin America. In return, they were expected to applaud the nation-building efforts of the ruling party. This policy produced some odd results, as during the late 1990s when many leftist academics received government grants to publish tracts in support of the Zapatista rebels.

The PRI's success in co-opting its critics, extending its corporatist networks into every sphere of society and its ability to maintain peace within the party by rotating power every sexenio, meant that Mexico was largely spared the political instability that plagued other Latin American countries in the 1960s and 70s. Mexico's staunch friendship with Fidel Castro's Cuba meant that Mexican leftist guerrilla groups were denied Cuban support, making it difficult for them to grow.

Although guerrilla struggle is a Mexican tradition stretching from the Chichimecas to Hidalgo, Juárez, Villa, and Zapata, the armed groups that arose in Mexico in recent decades were small and militarily weak, and were easily crushed by the army. After the Tlatelolco massacre, for instance, fifteen armed *focos* (groups) sprang up in the north and south of the nation. The 1974 army ambush of rural Guerrero school teacher Lucio Cabañas

Armed guards march in Mexico City.   *(Robert Francis/ South American pictures)*

and his "Party of the Poor" fighters put a swift end to left-wing insurgency for that decade.

A group called the Insurgent People's Revolutionary Army (ERPI) is one of a handful of tiny, armed movements that still survive today in poor, violent states like Guerrero. But the arrival of pluralist democracy in Mexico has made armed revolt illegitimate and even less likely to garner popular support.

The uprising by the Zapatistas Army of National Liberation (EZLN) on New Year's Day, 1994, was different. Although it began as an armed insurrection – fighting lasted for twelve days, killing 145 people – a cease-fire was soon established that has held to the present day.

The Zapatistas soon realized that their media skills offered them greater reach and influence than their feeble military capabilities. The rebels used the Internet – and the communication skills of their telegenic leader, Subcomandante Marcos – to transform themselves into a global movement, the world's first postmodern insurgency, promoting their indigenous rights agenda far more powerfully than they ever could have done as a purely military group. A permanent contingent of foreign NGO workers, anti-globalization activists, leftist radicals, and assorted hangers-on from Europe and North America settled into the Zapatista stronghold of La Realidad in the Lacandón jungle, forming a more effective shield against the Mexican army than an armored division.

Under President Ernesto Zedillo, a congressional commission negotiated a peace treaty with the rebels called the San Andrés Accords. They would have granted indigenous people broad cultural and political autonomy, judicial self-rule, and control over land and natural resources. But the Zedillo government refused to submit it for congressional ratification, and his government embarked on a tacit policy to isolate and ignore the rebels. During much of the Zedillo *sexenio*, they languished in their jungle stronghold as their public support ebbed away.

The arrival in office of Vicente Fox opened up new opportunities for Zapatistas. President Fox embraced the rebel cause, and quickly submitted the original San Andrés Accord to Congress in the form of a sweeping indigenous rights bill. In response, the Zapatistas embarked on an unarmed two-week bus tour of Mexico, culminating in an unprecedented appearance by rebel leaders before Congress to lobby for swift passage of the bill. The tour was a success, not only winning broad public sympathy for the indigenous cause, but laying the foundations for turning the Zapatistas into a Mexico-wide political movement through the self-styled National Indigenous Congress.

Ultimately, Congress approved a more limited version of the bill, balancing autonomy against national sovereignty, unity and individual rights. Although it was denounced by the Zapatistas, it held out the possibility that native Mexicans would achieve at least a strong measure of the cultural and political autonomy and legal recognition they had sought.

The Zapatistas forced the plight of indigenous Mexicans onto the national agenda, forcing a debate on issues that had long been swept under carpet. But the rebel's leading spokesman, Subcomandante Marcos, remains a controversial and divisive figure on the Mexican political scene. The man behind the ski mask was long ago identified as a white, middle-class former university lecturer named Rafael Sebastián Guillén Vicente. Even Mexicans sympathetic to the indigenous cause are wary of Marcos – for the cult of personality he fostered among his followers, for his Marxist leanings, his hunger for publicity, and his scorn for representative democracy.

Nor can the rebels boast of a sterling record of respect for human rights. Indigenous people living under Zapatista control in so-called "autonomous municipalities" are denied basic civil rights and freedoms. Expulsions of non-Zapatista residents from areas of rebel control have been common. The use of teenage soldiers has also tarnished the rebels' image: Mexicans recall that during the early stage of the uprising, the Zapatista leadership sent teenagers armed with dummy wooden rifles to the slaughter, by ordering them into battle against the Mexican army.

The Political Parties

The electoral opposition has come from both sides of the political aisle. In response to Cárdenas' allegedly Bolshevik policies, Catholic bankers founded the National Action Party in 1939. The PAN won its first federal deputies in the 1940s and for decades provided the only focus of opposition to the PRI in provincial towns and cities. The PAN gained converts in the conservative business community following López Portillo's 1982 nationalization of the banking system and the next year the party won a series of victories in municipal elections in the north. The new recruits, such as Manuel Clouthier, chairman of the nation's most conservative business chamber and later a National Action presidential candidate, were dubbed neo-PANistas, and their confrontational style shook up the staid middle-class party. The disputed 1985 election for Chihuahua's governor sparked street rioting by PANistas and a refusal by Catholic bishops to pronounce Mass until the balloting was cleaned up.

Three years later, the PRI and the PAN entered into a marriage of convenience designed to isolate the powerful center-left Cárdenas coalition and reduce Mexico's suddenly pluralistic politics to a single bipartisan consensus. In 1989, the PAN was awarded its first governorship (in Baja California Norte) and by late 1995 occupied four governor's mansions and governed a third of the population. On 2 July 2000, it won the presidency.

Many Mexicans think of the PAN as a party of prim churchgoers and conservative businessmen. In states and cities it governs, the party's prudishness has found expression in efforts to censor bra ads on billboards, punish women who wear short skirts to work, and ban a popular male strip show. For most of its 62-year history, the party was largely untouched by scandal, mainly because so few of its politicians actually held power. That has begun to change.

Although President Vicente Fox is a member of the PAN, he is an outsider in his own party – a maverick in cowboy boots and denim shirts who began his campaign for the presidency two years before the election, and imposed himself on the party by dint of his powerful media presence and outsize personality. Fox, who created his own independent campaign machine, came into office with few political debts to the PAN. He gave relatively few cabinet posts to its members, putting together instead a coalition government made up chiefly of businessmen and politicians from other parts of the political spectrum.

For much of the past decade, the left side of the electoral spectrum has been dominated by Cuauhtémoc Cárdenas' efforts to rekindle the Mexican Revolution. Expelled in 1987 from the party his father had consolidated, Cárdenas enlisted the support of tiny, left-sounding "satellite" parties (originally set up by the PRI-run government to perpetuate a false image of

Mexican political pluralism). After the fraud-marred 1988 presidential elections, Cárdenas founded the Party of the Democratic Revolution (PRD), a fusion of ex-PRIstas who deserted the ruling party with Cárdenas and a dozen different left tendencies (including the long-defunct communist party). In the first decade following its formation, the PRD was the subject of intense vilification by the PRI and the PAN, repeatedly faced electoral fraud, and has lost hundreds of its members to political violence.

But in recent years, the PRD has suffered even more from its own political miscalculations and missteps. An internal election in 1999 was marred by allegations of fraud, tarnishing the party's reputation for probity. Many of its leading lights defected, in despair over the movement's inability to transform itself from a fractious coalition of pressure groups into a coherent political party.

Cárdenas' popularity suffered grievously during the two years he was mayor of Mexico City, in which his administration seemed powerless to tackle the endemic crime, poverty, and mismanagement afflicting the Western hemisphere's largest metropolis. The dour and un-charismatic Cárdenas, whose lack of political skills became particularly evident during his City Hall tenure, seemed equally incapable of claiming credit for what he did accomplish – namely, launching reforms of the corrupt police force, cleaning up the city's finances, and funding grassroots initiatives to help the disadvantaged.

The 2000 election was a disaster for the party. Cárdenas, running for president for the third time, misread the mood of the voters and ran on a populist, anti-free trade, anti-globalization platform – in a nation that has seen significant benefits from NAFTA. He came in a distant third, with barely 17 percent of the vote – effectively ending his public political career at the age of 66.

His party fared little better. It lost congressional seats, reducing it to a rump in both houses. It lost its majority in the Mexico City legislative assembly, and lost control of several of the city's most important *delegaciónes* (districts).

The one bright spot for the PRD was that it held on to City Hall. Cardenas' heir-apparent within the party – Manuel Lopez Obrador, a rabble-rousing populist and former PRIsta from state of Tabasco – became mayor of Mexico City. With the next presidential elections due in 2006, the pugnacious *Tabasqueño* is the most formidable political figure in the opposition to Fox.

But the party remains afflicted with a profound crisis of identity. Founded by Cárdenas to embody his almost messianic crusade against the PRI, it seems directionless now that the hated ruling party has fallen from power. A split has emerged between militant leftists who are implacably hostile to President Fox, and moderates who call for the party to re-launch itself as a modern social-democratic movement that could appeal to Mexico's growing middle-class. But the PRD has seemed unable to craft a new political identity for itself in the democratic era.

The Cárdenas dynasty lives on, however. Cárdenas himself continues to yield behind-the-scenes influence as a party kingmaker, and his son Lázaro Cárdenas II is poised to win the governorship in the family's home state of Michoacán.

Mexico's newest opposition party is, of course, the PRI. Its 2000 electoral defeat dealt the party an enormous blow. "The Revolutionary Family," as the PRI elite was known, never had a coherent ideology to bind it together; chameleon-like, it shifted from populist statism to free-market globalism as circumstances dictated. Power was the only glue that held together the party's disparate factions and regional barons, that kept American-educated technocrats under the same roof as the thuggish old-style machine politicians known as the "dinosaurs."

Without power, the party began to unravel. It began losing state elections – first in Chiapas, then in Yucatán, both former bastions of the ruling party. Defections drained party's senior ranks. Influence within the party shifted to the "regional barons," the state governors.

No one could agree on why the party had lost power. The dinosaurs blamed the free-market reforms and political opening pursued by the last three PRI presidents, all technocrats – Miguel de la Madrid, Carlos Salinas, and Ernesto Zedillo. The moderates blamed corruption and economic mismanagement for the party's decline.

With the PRI still holding power in 18 of Mexico's 32 states, and in hundreds of municipalities, and with the largest numbers of seats in Congress, it is far from a spent force. But the search for a new role in the political landscape has not gone smoothly. Rudderless and lacking a clear ideology, predictions abound that the PRI may break up, perhaps leading to the creation of a new political entity based on the moderate core of the old one.

Distinct from the PRD, although providing a large slice of its supporters, is what has become known as "civil society," comprising the plethora of non-governmental organizations spanning everything from independent labor unions and farmers' organizations to university students, intellectuals, Christian base communities, housing associations, and Mexico's embattled gay and lesbian community. A growing role is played by human rights defenders, whose increasing independence forced the Salinas government to create the National Human Rights Commission (CNDH) in 1990. Such leaders as Rosario Ibarra, whose "Eureka" group demands the resolution of more than 500 political "disappearances" over the past twenty years, challenge the impunity of the security forces. More than 300 such groups now monitor human rights violations in Mexico.

Although some degree of political involvement had always taken place, the key catalyst in the upsurge of civil society was the Mexico City earthquake on 19 September 1985. The government's inability to function in the earthquake's wake forced inner city residents to take up the tasks of recovery, rescuing victims (*damnificados*), directing traffic, expropriating property from absentee landlords, and organizing huge mobilizations that forced President Miguel De la Madrid to build replacement housing.

Women were particularly active in the *damnificado* movement. Although women's associations were active in Madero's liberal campaign to topple Díaz and women later participated in the revolution as a contingent in Zapata's army, they were not granted the right to vote until 1954. Feminism in Mexico has been late in coming and is largely a middle-class US import. But the needs of a rapidly modernizing society and an emerging economy have brought increasing numbers of women into the workforce. Women now make up 48 percent of university students and a growing proportion of professionals and white-collar workers.

Since the 1985 earthquake, a burgeoning Mexican feminist movement has tried to bridge the gap with the grassroots. One example has been the 19 September Garment Workers Union, whose struggle to survive the devastating quake has been championed by the feminist writer Elena Poniatowska. The uprising by the Zapatista Army of National Liberation, in which women comprise a third of the fighting force and are leaders of the General Command, has inspired women to seize initiative in indigenous communities, where the selling of young girls, the practice of men taking several wives and domestic violence are common.

Civil society continues to be vocal, but its energies are not confined to electoral participation. It continues to fill Mexico City's zócalo, demonstrating its solidarity whenever social tensions reach boiling point, such as in the 1994 Zapatista rebellion.

Keeping the Peace

The Mexican military was the real winner of the revolution and prides itself as a revolutionary institution. The ballet between military and civilian authority fills chapters of Mexican history. Regionalized military insurrections troubled every president until Cárdenas, and maverick generals intervened in the elections of 1940 and 1952. But since the 1920s the military has not seized power, the longest coup-free epoch in Latin America.

Traditionally, relations between the military and the president are intricate and nuanced. They depend on each other's loyalty for survival.

In exchange for staying in the barracks, the military is awarded power and autonomy – the military hierarchy chooses Mexico's secretary of defense and the navy (a general and an admiral are always appointed), and runs its own industries, justice, and commercial systems. The military's decisions obey self-interest and the top brass' internal logic. Budgets are traditionally kept small – Mexico's defense spending as a share of GDP (around 1 percent) is among the lowest in Latin America – but the president allots unspecified discretionary funds to supplement military spending. A tradition of secrecy and lack of civilian oversight remain an integral part of military culture.

The army, navy, and air force have a total of 175,000 troops, the vast majority young, unschooled recruits drawn from the rural and urban poor, many of them Indians, for whom the military provides a steady job, a structured life, and opportunity for economic advancement.

Constitutionally, the president is the commander-in-chief and is surrounded by a military guard known in Spanish as the *Estado Mayor*. The Estado Mayor, which is drawn from all three services, has grown in prestige to become a quasi-independent and influential group within the military hierarchy.

The Mexican army dominates the services with 120,000 troops. The navy is largely a ceremonial corps, although it is also charged with drug interdiction on the high seas and protecting Caribbean offshore oil platforms. The air force is the youngest and fastest-growing service, and is scheduled to become independent of the secretary of defense. The air force received much of the US$750 million in military equipment that the Pentagon sold or licensed to Mexico from 1982 to 1992.

As an instrument of national defense, in theory the military is charged with defending Mexico from its neighbor to the north. The United States has invaded three times (although the last was in 1916, when General Pershing chased Villa through the Chihuahua desert), and a scenario for invasion from the north is still taught at the national military college. Mexico's grim experience of foreign intervention on its soil has fostered a strong isolationist streak. It contributes no troops to UN peacekeeping, and has never intervened abroad, except for the largely symbolic contribution of a single air fighter squadron – the legendary *Escuadron 201* – to the US forces in the Pacific during World War II.

As the economies of the United States and Mexico have converged, so have security interests. With 2,000 miles of border separating the two nations, Mexico is a major national security issue for Washington – oil supplies, drug traffic, immigration, and political unrest are crucial items on the bilateral agenda. The Pentagon woos Mexico's generals with aircraft, ground vehicles, and technology, designated for use in the military's

MEXICO

Mexico combines political stability and revolution. The ruling Institutional Revolutionary party has been in power since 1929, yet revolution and protest is also part of the Mexican tradition

Mural rendition of the Aztec capital Tenochitlán
(Tony morrison South American Pictures)

Superbarrio, a larger than life figure in a wrestlers costume, leads support for a teachers' strike in Mexico City
(Julio Etchart/ Reportage)

Revolutionaries guard a train during the Mexican Revolution, 1910-1917
(Pedro Martinez/ South American Pictures)

Mexico's rich cultural expression combines both pre-Columbian and hispanic influences in a unique style, best expressed in the murals which adorn walls from government buildings to the poorest slums

A huge twenty ton stone head of the ancient Olmec culture, Villahermosa.
(Robert Francis/ South American Pictures)

The murals of Diego Rivera, painted shortly after the Mexican Revolution, are perhaps the best known works of Mexican art.
(Mike Roy)

The mural tradition is still vibrant, as in this example from Ciudad Juárez, on the US-Mexican border.
(Julio Etchart/Reportage)

Mexico has the largest indigenous population in the Americas, descendants of its numerous pre-Columbian civilisations. Despite the official rhetoric praising Mexico's indigenous traditions, indigenous peoples are the poorest section of the population

Fruit seller in the market in Juchitán, Oaxaca.
(Steve Bowles/Survival International)

Tarahumara Indian from Chihuahua, northern Mexico.
(Steve Bowles/Survival International)

'Conquest of Mexico', Diego Rivera mural in the Cortes Palace, Cuemavaca
(Tony Morrison/ South American Pictures)

Built on the site of the Aztec capital Tenochtitlán, Mexico City is the largest city in the world and a place of stark contrasts between ancient and modern, riches and poverty, and high and low cultural forms

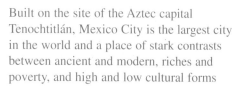

Modern-day street market in the *zócalo*, or main square of Mexico City.
(Tony Morrison/South American Pictures)

Indigenous women selling cloth dolls in Mexico City.
(Tony Morrison/South American Pictures)

Mexico City stock exchange.
(Julio Etchart/Reportage)

Shantytowns in the capital's industrial belt.
(Julio Etchart/Reportage)

anti-drug campaigns (aircraft intended for the drug war were used against the Zapatista rebels in January 1994).

Although charged with national security, the absence of an invading army has made keeping its own people in line the military's main mission. The 1968 Tlatelolco massacre, for which the military continues to shirk the blame, permanently stained the institution's honor, and many Mexicans have never felt comfortable with the military since.

Under the PRI, whenever the president needed to impress his political will upon the nation, the Mexican military has been at his disposal, intervening in strikes, elections, and civil prosecutions. It is the prime suspect in the abduction, torture, or murder of hundreds of anti-government activists in recent decades.

But the most controversial aspect of the military's role has been its involvement in law enforcement and the fight against drug trafficking. Evidence is overwhelming that the armed forces have been providing protection to traffickers. Six Mexican generals have been jailed since 1997 on charges of being in the pay of drug lords, including the former chief of Mexico's anti-drug efforts, General Jesús Gutiérrez Rebollo, whose story was dramatized in the Oscar-winning film *Traffic*.

The military polishes its image by engaging in disaster relief and ecological activities, such as planting trees, while "social labor" campaigns bring doctors, dentists, and barbers into rural villages. But the Mexican military's real job is fighting, not pulling teeth. During counterinsurgency campaigns against both the Zapatistas and Cabañas' group in the 1970s, the military was accused of abusing civilian populations. More recently, it stands accused of torturing and falsely imprisoning a pair of environmental activists, Rodolfo Montiel and Teodoro Cabrera, who were protesting illegal logging in the state of Guerrero.

In effort to address these concerns, President Fox chose a politically independent ex-senator, Adolfo Aguilar Zinser, as the country's first national security advisor, charging him with revamping the country's security doctrine. The irony of the appointment is striking: Zinser himself was once briefly abducted by the army in 1984 after publicly criticizing the government's treatment of Guatemalan refugees.

Zinser is also dedicated to dismantling the vast intelligence networks set up by the PRI to spy on its political opponents and critics. Illegal wiretapping and electronic surveillance – mainly but not exclusively carried out by the country's spy agency, the Center for Information on National Security – was used to intimidate opposition leaders, newspaper editors, reporters, and union leaders. In the past, bugging equipment was found in the national human rights commission, several state supreme court chambers and in the offices of prominent opposition politicians – including then-candidate Vicente Fox and the man who is currently his interior minister, Santiago Creel.

The Criminal Police

A measure of the dismal condition of human rights in Mexico: it is the world's leading importer of torture instruments, including leg irons and straitjackets, according to Amnesty International. And the Mexican police are the worst offenders. "The police regularly obtain information through torture, prosecutors use this evidence in courts, and the courts continue to admit as evidence confessions extracted under torture," according to the US State Department.

Reform of the country's notoriously corrupt, brutal, and ineffectual law enforcement bodies has long been on the political agenda. But the challenges are formidable. The inter-relationship of cops and robbers in Mexico is historic – Porfirio Díaz emptied Mexico City's prisons of its worst criminals to form the city's public police force. Today there are dozens of police agencies in Mexico, ranging from municipal forces to national security agents of the Center for Intelligence and National Security (CISEN), who often compete for jurisdiction and spoils.

The most feared agents are the state and federal judicial police. Attached to public justice ministries, *judiciales* investigate and apprehend suspects assigned to them by the courts and are often accused of framing them. Agents are abetted by *madrinas* (literally, "godmothers"), criminal elements who function as informers and bounty hunters. The use of torture to extract confessions is routine. The National Human Rights Commission (CNDH) censures repressive *judiciales*, who are sometimes sacked, but mass firings of police agents have proved ineffective, because ex-agents join the gangs of the criminals they were once assigned to capture. Worse, delays in setting up a national police database mean that a corrupt cop fired in one city can easily get re-hired in the police force of another.

Judicial agents are only in on the ground floor of the extreme corruption that pervades Mexican police structures. It is commonplace for police commanders and prosecutors to buy positions in lucrative urban and border zones. Bribes, known as *mordidas* and *chayotes*, guarantee impunity for the powerful. A police career is widely seen as a path to power, money, and women. Many cops spend much of their time collecting "rents" – i.e. extortion money – from unregistered businesses on their beats, from which they pay a percentage to their commanding officers. Honest cops who refuse to make these payments are given the worst jobs, and many eventually leave the force in despair.

Mexican police are also notoriously inefficient. In Mexico City, only four percent of reported crimes are ever solved, even though the Mexican capital has more police per person than most other large cities. Mexico City has 64 police for every 10,000 people, compared to 25 for London.

Efforts to reform the police have focused on providing better pay – to reduce the incentives for corruption – and better training, given that many existing police have only rudimentary schooling and scant knowledge of the law. Mexico City under the PRD has led the way, raising starting pay for judicial police to about $1,000 a month – a middle-class wage in Mexico that is attracting large numbers of university graduates to law enforcement. A former human rights advocate heads the city's police training academy.

On a national level, the Fox government has sought to re-organize the judicial apparatus so as to separate law enforcement from the attorney general's office, and to consolidate the newly-created Federal Preventative Police, loosely modeled on America's Federal Bureau of Investigation.

A long-time human rights campaigner, Mariclaire Acosta, was hired by the Fox administration to mastermind a government campaign that will target the two worst areas of abuse: the routine use of torture to extract confessions, and the practice of holding suspects in detention for up to two years before they get a chance to appear at a probable-cause hearing.

There are also plans to set up a transparency commission, similar to the truth commissions in Argentina, Chile, and South Africa, to investigate past abuses. Visas are no longer being denied to international monitors like Amnesty International and Human Rights Watch, and harassment of local groups like the Augustin Pro Human Rights Center has ended. Whether these moves toward greater openness and accountability can overcome the resistance of an entrenched bureaucracy and a political class reluctant to re-open the wounds of the past is an open question.

The Dysfunctional Courts

Far-reaching change will eventually require reform of the dysfunctional and grossly inefficient legal system.

Corruption is rife in the judiciary, where low pay and poor legal training are endemic. Judgments and rulings aren't enforced. Because of excessive caseloads, many judges don't even preside in person over their trials. Routine civil cases like divorces and lawsuits can drag on for years. Loopholes and ambiguities in the law mean that cases of petty theft are punished more harshly than large-scale graft and embezzlement, reinforcing the belief that the powerful enjoy impunity.

Laws are badly drafted and often contradictory, and often non-existent in areas that are crucial to the functioning of a democratic society: For example, Mexico has no freedom of information law (although the Fox government is planning one), making it difficult to hold the state accountable for its actions. Existing laws are vague or full of loopholes in many other important areas – consumer protection, the accountability of public officials, fiduciary responsibility of banks toward their customers, protection of minority shareholders and the freedom of the press.

The Supreme Court is supposed to protect constitutional rights, but its past rulings often served to bolster the authoritarian system under the PRI – like a ruling in 1992 that conferred tacit legitimacy on the use of police torture, by making a suspect's initial statement in police custody the only one considered legally valid.

Even in recent years, as the Court has grown more independent, its rulings tend to be too narrow and restrictive to have any wider application in the protection of civil rights. Partly this is a function of Mexico's civil law system, which invests supreme authority in the specific language of the law – unlike the Anglo-American common law system, in which the application of laws is dictated by accumulated precedents of individual court rulings. In the Anglo-American system, respect for the law is seen as a common good; in Mexico's civil law system, the law is seen as simply another tool by which the authorities impose their will on society.

Mexicans whose rights have been violated have only one avenue of recourse – the *amparo directo* – which allows an individual to challenge an action of the authorities, such an arrest or court ruling, on the grounds that his or her constitutional rights have been abused. The *amparo* is one of the few areas of the Mexican judicial system that functions reasonably well; the others are the electoral and tax tribunals, as well as the privately-run Mexico Arbitration Center for resolving business conflicts.

The legal system as a whole is poorly prepared to face one of its biggest emerging challenges: disputes arising from Mexico's federal system. Under the PRI, Mexico was federal in name only; power was so centralized that President Carlos Salinas was able to dismiss 17 of the country's 32 state governors during his reign.

But the transition to democracy has unleashed long-simmering tensions, as states begin to mount challenges to the federal government over the division of powers, the allocation of budget funds and tax collection. Worse, legal conflicts between states are likely to grow as well: some 60 potential disputes over demarcation of state borders are pending. Unlike mature federations like Canada, which has decades of constitutional litigation under its belt, Mexico's judicial system has virtually no experience in this area.

"So Far From God."

When, in 1988, the heads of the Mexican Catholic Church attended the inauguration of President Carlos Salinas wearing clerical collars, society was scandalized. Priests – even Cardinals – were prohibited by the Constitution from wearing clerical garb in public. Participation in politics, including voting, was forbidden. The Church could not conduct legal marriages or run its own schools, although it quite openly did so, (three recent Mexican presidents attended Catholic schools). Most of these prohibitions were the legacy of Juárez's 1857 constitution, embedded in Carranza's 1917 magna carta.

Jacobin reaction is an understudied current in Mexican history. Anti-Roman Catholic virulence is rooted in the colony. The Church was (and remains) a great landowner and its lending practices were tantamount to usury. After Independence, the hierarchy stood with the ruling elite and welcomed a foreign emperor to Mexican shores. During the Porfiriato, the Church exercised dominion over a nation of sinners. "Poor Mexico, so close to the United States and so far from God," bemoaned the dictator Díaz.

Jacobin persecution of the Catholic Church culminated in Calles' *Cristiada*. On the night in 1926 that churches were to be closed in Mexico City, cathedrals and parish chapels were filled to overflowing. The revolt reached its zenith in 1928 when a Catholic zealot, José Toral, assassinated the *caudillo* Alvaro Obregón. In the provinces, priests were rounded up and imprisoned. Tabasco Governor Tomás Garrido Canabal ordered that there could be only one priest for every 30,000 worshippers – and that priest must be married. The anti-clerical persecutions inspired novelist Graham Greene to write *The Power and The Glory*.

The religiosity of Mexicans is palpable. On Sundays, the Basilica of the Virgin of Guadalupe in Mexico City swarms with pilgrims, as do the ancient ruins at Teotihuacán just a few miles further north. The vast majority – 88.2 percent – of Mexicans profess the Catholic faith; each year is punctuated by Church feasts and saints' days. At the grassroots, the popular Church flourishes, worshipping thinly-disguised indigenous deities and canonizing lay saints like Jesús Malverde, a Robin Hood-like bandit who has become the patron of *contrabandistas* (smugglers), with a shrine by the railroad tracks in Culiacán, Sinaloa.

The faithful's passionate devotion contrasts with a hierarchy that is as secretive and insular as the military. At the top of Church structure is the Mexican Episcopal Conference or CEM, which groups together the nation's 109 Cardinals, Archbishops, Bishops, and auxiliaries. The Cardinal of Mexico City ministers to the largest diocese in the Roman Catholic world (17 million faithful), including the Basilica, the Mexican Church's biggest money-maker. Other cardinals reign in Guadalajara and Monterrey; Juan Jesús Posadas, the Cardinal of Guadalajara, was allegedly caught up in a shoot-out between drug gangs and killed in May 1993 (although most Mexicans, including the Church, reject the story, and there is evidence he was the target of assassination by drug barons).

Pope John Paul II has visited Mexico four times in the last two decades and the Papal Nuncio (the Vatican ambassador) is one of the most powerful presences in the hierarchy of Mexico's Church. He influences all Church appointments and combats liberation theology, a minority strain within the conservative CEM.

Despite the "black legend" of the Conquest, in which the Church was blamed for the slaughter of the Indians and the destruction of their cultures, the hierarchy has always harbored prelates who insist the Indians have souls worth saving. Bartolomé de las Casas, the first Bishop of Chiapas (1540–46), who traveled to the Americas with Columbus, recorded the agony of the *indígenas* and freed them from slavery, advocating that blacks from Africa be imported to take the Indians' place (the Bishop later repented this error).

In contrast to the conservative hierarchy, the lower ranks of the clergy have been in the forefront of the struggle for social justice throughout Mexican history – Hidalgo and Morelos are only the best known. The radical 1968 Medellín Council of Latin American Bishops left the imprint of liberation theology upon the Mexican Church. Under the guidance of "Red" Bishop Sergio Méndez Arceo, the Cuernavaca diocese became a hotbed of Catholic radicalism in the 1960s. Two Méndez disciples – Bishop Arturo Lona in Tehuantepec, Oaxaca, and Bishop Samuel Ruiz in San Cristóbal, Chiapas (de las Casas' diocese) for years represented the "Church of the Poor" within the CEM. A network of 15,000 Christian base communities, boasting 150,000 activists, stretches across central and southern Mexico.

Under the Salinas policy of *rapprochement*, Constitutional Articles 3 and 130 were modified to give the Church legal standing and renewed political rights. Diplomatic relations with the Vatican, broken off by Juárez, were resumed. Yet Jacobin resentment has continued to simmer, leading some Catholic Bishops to suggest that Cardinal Posadas' murder was engineered by such forces of reaction.

The constitutional amendment has sparked increased participation in politics by the Church. Jesuit, Dominican, and diocesan centers have become important players in the growing human rights movement, while bishops are no longer bashful about making political statements from the pulpit.

The election of Vicente Fox, a fervent Catholic who makes no secret of his piety, aroused expectations that his PAN government would go even further in satisfying Church demands for influence in society – for example, by re-instituting religious education in public schools. Although

Stall near the shrine of the Virgin of Guadalupe, Mexico City. *(Carlos Reyes-Manzo/ Andes Press Agency)*

Fox broke taboos by going to pray at the Basilica on the day of his inauguration, he made it clear that the status quo would remain by appointing a former *PRIsta* as his secretary of religious affairs.

Mexican protestantism favored the Jacobin cause. The "historical churches" of the Presbyterians, Methodists, Baptists, and Anglicans were favored by Juárez, a Freemason, whose image is still venerated by Mexico's Protestants. In 1919, US missionaries developed the "Cincinnati Plan" that divided post-revolutionary Mexico into *zones* of evangelization, while Obregón invited Mennonites to settle the Chihuahua desert in 1923. Lázaro Cárdenas, another Freemason, invited Protestant missionaries to work in the rural outback in an effort to break the Catholics' hold on the countryside.

Evangelicals and charismatics are the spearhead of the Protestant thrust, representing the fastest-growing faiths in Mexico. Tirelessly knocking on doors in the poorest colonies, evangelicals fill storefront churches while nearby cathedrals sit empty. The protestants attract converts with a strict interpretation of the gospel, sobriety, and no strictures against birth control. Evangelical churches are concentrated along the northern and southern borders, where ministries from the US and Guatemala (the most protestantized Latin country) establish beachheads. In the southern border state of Tabasco, the Protestant population is expected to outnumber the Catholic early in the 21st century. They have also made great inroads in poor states like Chiapas, where the Catholic Church never cultivated a purely indigenous clergy.

Challenged by the Protestant advance, the Catholic Church disdainfully calls the churches "sects," even suggesting they are agents of US imperialism. Sporadic clashes have taken place between Catholic and Protestant communities, most dramatically in San Juan Chamula, a traditional indigenous community in the Chiapas highlands, where 25,000 evangelicals have been expelled from their land.

Farm and Factory

Although the body has moved to the city, Mexico's soul still resides in the countryside. Urban dwellers, now 75 percent of the population, nostalgically trace their roots back to the soil. *Ranchero* songs recall rural life with tenderness and longing.

The Mexican Revolution was an expression of the rage of the nation's landless *campesinos*, but the promises that accompanied that convoluted social upheaval remain largely unfulfilled. Now, as Mexico enters the global economy and imports vast stores of staples such as maize and beans, the agricultural sector is fading into history.

Despite its rich agrarian legacy, Mexico is a country whose topography is hardly suited to large-scale agricultural production. Half its land area is arid and semi-arid. Only twelve percent of its 487 million square acres has enough water for cultivation.

Land ownership is divided between communal and individual holdings. Twenty-eight thousand communal farms, known as *ejidos* (largely worked by mestizos) and indigenous *comunidades* are spread throughout the agricultural zones. Ejidos are owned by the community, but divided up between families for individual tilling. *Pequeños propietarios* (the sometimes euphemistic "small property owners") hold plots ranging from 40 acres up to 22,000-acre cattle ranches. The *latifundios* (large estates) that dominated agriculture before agrarian reform persist as landowners have divided up estates between members of their families or given their titles to *prestanombres* ("name-lenders") in order to get around the legal limits on ownership.

Agrarian reform enjoyed its finest hour during the Cárdenas era. Each subsequent presidency has watered down the nation's commitment to its campesinos.

Land is often distributed for political gain, as presidents hand out certificates for waterless tracts to *ejidatarios*. Between 1952 and 1982, 85 percent of the land handed out (the *reparto*) was unsuitable for cultivation. When José López Portillo (1976–82), sought symbolically to end the *reparto* by moving Zapata's remains from Cuautla, Morelos to Mexico City's Monument of the Revolution (where Carranza, the mastermind behind Zapata's death, is buried), thousands of campesinos gathered

Modern-day Maya: Bartolomé Puuc and his
wife outside their home   *(Tony Morrison/South American Pictures)*

around the tomb of the Caudillo and fought off police agents assigned to retrieve his bones. The 1979 confrontation sparked an independent campesino movement, the National Coordinating Body of the Ayala Plan (CNPA) that survives today in numerous organizations sporting Emiliano Zapata's initials. The Zapatista Army of National Liberation (EZLN) is the best known example.

Under constant attack from security forces and the private armies of landowners ("white guards"), independent campesino groups seek to recover land that once belonged to their *ejido* or community and suffer imprisonment and death for their efforts. Between 1982 and 1988, 700 members of one such group were imprisoned in Chiapas alone.

The technocrats who have governed Mexico since 1982 view the *ejido* as a misguided experiment in statist agriculture that both failed to alleviate rural poverty and to provide the basis for modernizing small-holder farming. The passing on of *ejido* land from one generation to the next has fragmented holdings, so that 60 percent of Mexico's three million e*jidatarios* now farm plots of five acres or less. Declining production has made Mexico one of the world's four largest grain importers – a fifth of the corn now consumed comes from outside the country, a total that is increasing under NAFTA. The last nail in the coffin for Mexico's campesinos was the Salinas administration's 1991 revision of Constitutional Article 27, ending the *reparto* and promoting the sale and renting of *ejido* lands to private capital and agribusiness.

Now, as globalization continues apace, cornland in the south is taken over by cattle ranchers with McDonald's contracts, and irrigated land in the north is turned over to export crops, including strawberries, asparagus, broccoli, jalapeño chili peppers, grapes, nuts, peaches, chickpeas, olives, cucumbers and watermelon. Mexico produces one of every three tomatoes and a quarter of all melons consumed in the US. The country's farm exports have quadrupled in the past decade to $4.15 billion a year. They represent the other face of Mexican agriculture: large, modern, efficient, industrial-sized farms that are increasingly managed according to foreign methods and foreign standards. They are one of the undisputed successes of the post-NAFTA era; but at the same time, they have highlighted the dismal failure to improve the conditions of Mexico's millions of small farmers.

Displaced campesinos have been abandoning the family farm and flooding the cities in search of work for generations, but few have managed to join the industrial workforce and fewer still, its organized sector. Of a 38 million-member urban workforce, about 10 million workers belong to trade unions – most of them affiliated with the PRI.

Old-Style Unions Persevere

The dominant labor organization continues to be the Confederation of Mexican Workers (CTM), which encompasses 14,000 separate unions, many limited to a single workplace, a fragmentation that hinders industry-wide solidarity. The CTM, which claims 5.5 million workers, along with four smaller labor federations, traditionally formed one leg of the PRI's corporate structure.

The other two main pillars of PRI corporatist support were the National Confederation of Popular Organizations (representing street vendors, taxi drivers, transport workers, and civil servants) and the National Campesino Confederation (representing peasant farmers).

The PRI relied heavily on the support of its corporatist allies. In exchange for turning out the vote, the CTM and its allies were allotted a quota of seats in the Mexican Congress, though this practice was eventually phased out.

PRI-affiliated union bosses are known as *charros* (flamboyantly-dressed cowboys), ruling through coercion and negotiating contracts behinds the backs of their membership. Workplace militancy is discouraged by the charros. Goon squads are dispatched to break up unauthorized wildcat strikes, such as the confrontations at a Ford plant near Mexico City in 1991. Legal strikes are rare. In 1989, Carlos Salinas ordered the military to dissolve a miners' strike at Cananea, Sonora, where a bloody 1906 strike in defiance of US owners gave birth to the Mexican labor movement. The mine was subsequently privatized.

The political influence of the unions went into decline in the 1990s, as union bosses gradually lost control over their members' votes. Indeed, in the 2000 election the powerful oil workers' union voted overwhelmingly for Vicente Fox – one of many organized labor bastions to switch allegiance to the opposition.

But even while their political patrons in Mexico City have lost power, the old PRI-loyal charros retain their influence in the workplace. With their ability to mobilize their members in strikes and work-disrupting protests, they remain a force to be reckoned with. Labor reforms may eventually weaken their power bases. A recent decision by the Supreme Court allows independent unions to compete on the shop floor with official ones, though it will be difficult to put into practice. One of the most powerful tools against the power of the old union bosses – the secret ballot – is still virtually unknown on Mexican shop floors.

The threat of losing one's job is the most effective way of quieting labor unrest. Labor secretariat statistics count only 2.3 percent of the economically-active population as unemployed, but the true number of un- and underemployed workers is as high as 33 percent, according to UNAM economist José Luis Calva. Mexico has no system of unemployment benefits and those without jobs are forced into the informal sector to survive.

Those with jobs are not doing much better. Workers lost over half their buying power in the "lost decade" of the 1980s, and were also hit hard by the 1994 peso crisis. Economists predict that the entry of China into the World Trade Organization will put further downward pressure on wages in Mexico, and that the country will actually begin to lose low-wage jobs to Chinese factories. This fear is behind government efforts to encourage the growth of higher-skilled, high valued-added manufacturing to gradually take the place of the low-wage assembly plants. Some state governments, like those of Nuevo Leon and Jalisco, actually discourage investors from setting up new maquiladoras in their regions.

Despite the official labor movement's quiescence, some unions remain true to their principles. The electricians' union, SME, has a history of labor solidarity. The education workers' union, SNTE, with 800,000 members the largest single union in Latin America, has a vocal membership that has toppled the organization's charro leadership. The telephone workers, STRM, pride themselves on democratic structures and forcing adjustments to neo-liberal measures. When the telephone company, Telmex, was privatized by Salinas, the workers received 4.4 percent of its stock, making the STRM one of the wealthiest unions in Mexico.

But most labor militants are concentrated outside the mainstream. The Authentic Workers Front (FAT), with 70,000 members, has survived for 35 years as an independent federation. The 19 September Garment Workers Union was born from the 1985 Mexico City earthquake in which many sweatshop workers lost their lives. The Independent Proletarian Movement (MPI) organizes bus drivers and the impoverished *colonias* that they serve. Another potential force for change are US unions – such as the Teamsters, the United Electrical Workers (UE) and the AFL-CIO, as well as NGOs like the Worker Rights Consortium – that are crossing the border to organize and monitor Mexican workers at transnational corporations with which they have US contracts.

One starting point has been the maquiladoras that now employ 1.3 million workers, more twice as many as when NAFTA began. Recently, an NGO-led campaign won concessions for workers at Kukdong, a Korean clothing manufacturer in central Puebla state which supplies the Nike shoe company.

4. ECONOMY

Mexican Miracles, Booms, and Busts

If one is to believe Augustín Lagorreta, himself the scion of a prestigious banking family, the Mexican economy rests in the hands of just 300 movers and shakers. Whatever the precise dimensions of the ruling group, the concentration of capital shocks even the World Bank, which believes that Mexico has "one of the worst profiles of income distribution in the world." During the 1990s, inequality in wages increased more in Mexico than anywhere else in Latin America.

Wealth is concentrated in the three major cities, Monterrey, Guadalajara, and the Federal District (Mexico City), and is owned by private families and alliances of those families, known as *grupos*, many of which function as monopolies or near-monopolies: Telmex has 95 percent of the domestic calls market; Cintra owns both national airlines; state-run Pemex controls oil and gas; Bimbo dominates the bread and pastry market. In beer and cement, too, there is little competition.

Much like the Church and the military, the private sector had no formal place in the PRI-government hierarchy, but business and political leaders maintained an unwritten pact that ceded direction of Mexico's economic policies to entrepreneurial interests. President Fox has made the link more explicit by appointing business executives to senior cabinet positions, with the aim of bringing more managerial efficiency to the Mexican state.

Fox's economic reform agenda aims to cut the bureaucracy, revamp the notoriously byzantine tax system so that it both collects more revenue and eases burdens on business and incomes, reduce the government's dependence on volatile oil revenues, open up the energy industry to foreign investment, improve education and worker training, and ultimately accelerate economic growth to seven percent a year. It's a tall order. Even his PRI predecessor, Ernesto Zedillo, couldn't convince his own party to adopt many of these structural changes.

Today's dominant private sector contrasts with the policies of Lázaro Cárdenas, who saw the state as an "arbiter" directing the economy for the common good. Cárdenas feared the tendency of private capital to concentrate in the hands of the very few. But after the General's exit from office in 1940, such ideas got short shrift until the Echeverría era.

1946–70 are painted as the years of "the Mexican miracle," when the "import substitution" model encouraged national production and industry was subsidized and protected from outside competition by high import tariffs. During the "miracle" years, annual growth averaged six percent, domestic agriculture fed the nation, foreign debt stayed low, and price stability reigned. An urban middle-class emerged and the country industrialized. The 1968 Olympic Games, the first ever held in the developing world, was to have marked the emergence of Mexico as a candidate for first world status.

Economic and political misfortune often coalesce in Mexico. The Tlatelolco massacre on the eve of the 1968 Olympics revealed middle-class frustrations with authoritarian rule, and a deeper rage down below at having been cut out of the much-touted "miracle." By the end of the 1960s, that miracle was badly tattered. Farmers could no longer keep up with demand, and Mexico began importing food and, more significantly, oil, to keep industry producing. Growth slipped to zero by 1972, as worldwide recession further increased unemployment. Mexico's vaunted price stability fell victim to inflation.

Luis Echeverría (1970–76) moved the nation leftward with his populist, neo-Cardenista policies. "Shared development" would give the underclass a greater stake in the system and neutralize the radicals. Echeverría looked south, promoting third world solidarity against the yanqui imperialists, but even as he condemned the North, his government was borrowing heavily from US banks. The foreign debt jumped from US$4 billion to US$11 billion, but neo-Cardenista rhetoric and debt-led development could not halt the economic slide. Echeverría was forced to devalue the peso by 43 percent, the first devaluation in 20 years. The "Mexican miracle" was dead.

Taking power amid rumors of a military coup, Echeverría's successor, José López Portillo, was at first seen as a man of reason who could calm a business community upset not only by the poor performance of the economy but also because bankers and industrialists were being murdered by Marxist guerrillas in the country's major cities. López Portillo's carefully nurtured image as an antidote to Echeverría's populism disintegrated in 1977 when major oil deposits were discovered in the Sound of Campeche and Mexico's oil reserves swelled from 22 billion to 72 billion barrels, the sixth largest in the world.

Mexico's oil has a hallowed history. The Aztecs discovered *chapopote* near Poza Rica, Veracruz and offered it as incense to their deities. The Spanish caulked their ships with it. Porfirian-era capitalists such as James Doheny (US) and Weetman Pearson (UK) built wells, commercialized production, and controlled Mexico's oil industry well past the revolution. President Cárdenas wrested the industry back from the Anglo-American interlopers, igniting a nationalist flame in the Mexican bosom. Cárdenas viewed domestic production as essential to grease the wheels of Mexican industry, but oil has always been Mexico's pipeline to the global economy and after the second world war, exports took priority.

With the new oil finds, Pemex, the state oil company, was generating 50 percent more income than the next six Mexican industries combined. Most – 65 percent – of Pemex's income goes directly to the federal government and accounts for about a third of the annual budget. Flush with oil-dollars, the economy zoomed to eight percent annual growth between 1978 and 1981. As the oil boom took off, foreign lenders lined up at Pemex's door. Under López Portillo, the country went on a borrowing binge and foreign debt grew by US$60 billion.

"We have only to administer abundance," the jubilant president informed the nation after the Campeche finds. López's style was lavish. He introduced the SAM (Mexican Food System) program that paid farmers to produce cheap food for urban workers and gave the nation one brief year of nutritional self-sufficiency (1981). He also built kitsch monuments to indigenous culture such as the pink moonscape of the "Otomíe (Nahnu) Ceremonial Center" in Temoaya, Mexico state. Both Echeverría and López Portillo bailed out many failing businesses. Between 1970 and 1982, the number of state enterprises grew to 1,155.

The bad news began with steep oil price drops in October 1981. Mexican oil now accounted for 78 percent of all exports, most of it being shipped to the US. Falling oil revenues could not keep pace with payments on the escalating short-term debt. In August 1982, López Portillo's finance minister privately told his Washington counterpart that Mexico could no longer meet its foreign obligations, an announcement that marked the start of the Latin American debt crisis.

The debt crisis brought the boom to an end with a sickening thud. Capital flight grew to panic proportions as billions of dollars were pulled out of the country. In a desperate effort to halt the *"sacadolares"* (dollar pullers), López Portillo nationalized the banks, a Cárdenas-like stroke that infuriated the private sector.

Like Echeverría, José López Portillo left office in disgrace. Pressured to devalue an over-priced currency, the president bragged that he would instead defend the peso "like a dog." Ten days later, he ordered the first of three devaluations that sank the peso to more than a hundred to the dollar. Today, when the aging López Portillo appears in public, bystanders are apt to bark in derision.

NAFTA and the New World Order

The debt crisis and a plunge in oil prices – the government's main source of revenue back then – forced the government to launch an opening of the economy. Miguel de la Madrid (1982–88), the first of three "technocratic" presidents, had to pick up the pieces of the miracle-turned-debacle. Resolution of the debt crisis was the first order of business. In return for promises of fresh loans and being allowed to reschedule its debt repayments, Mexico embarked on structural reforms that would dismantle trade barriers, privatize state-run industries, and slash government spending to sustainable levels. The de la Madrid presidency coincided with *"la crisis,"* actually a series of crises with low points in 1983 and 1985 due to further slippage in oil prices. Despite an IMF austerity program, inflation soared to 150 percent by 1987. As workers lost 60 percent of their buying power, the foreign debt grew to US$107 billion, second highest in the developing world. Debt service alone took up half the nation's export income. Social services were slashed and by 1990, 41 million Mexicans, nearly half the population, were living beneath the poverty line.

Ringing in the death knell for Mexico's nationalist "import substitution" model of development, de la Madrid led Mexico into the General Agreement on Tariffs and Trade (GATT) in 1985. The president sold off nearly half the state enterprises acquired by his predecessors. In his final year in office, de la Madrid initiated the first of seven pacts between business, the government, and labor that held wages well below the inflation rate for years. The *pactos* signaled a continuation of free-market policies, as did de la Madrid's selection of Carlos Salinas de Gortari as his successor.

Salinas, who many Mexicans think stole the 1988 election from his opponent Cuauhtémoc Cárdenas by fraud, was an ambitious president, determined to embed free-market reforms so deeply in the Mexican economy that there could never again be any return to statist models. Upon assuming office, he met US President-elect George Bush to discuss US-Mexican economic integration, leading in 1990 to the proposal for a North America Free Trade Agreement (NAFTA), known in Spanish as the TLC (*Tratado de Libre Comercio*). NAFTA would stretch from "the Yukon to the Yucatán," capturing 360 million potential consumers.

To prepare for North American economic integration, (Canada, which has a separate free trade agreement with the US, was also included), Salinas altered Mexico's investment laws in 1989 to allow 100 percent foreign investment in every area of the economy except oil (foreign participation had been limited to 49 percent). He revised Constitutional Article 27 to allow the gradual privatization of the *ejido* system, encouraging foreign investment in Mexican agriculture. The balding, dynamic president (at 39, the youngest ever to assume office) sold off the national airlines and the telephone company to prominent donors to his election campaign and handed eighteen nationalized banks back to *grupos* of their former owners and newly-favored financiers. To curry favor with the White House, Salinas even increased petroleum shipments to the US during the 1991 Persian Gulf conflict, though a popular backlash forced him to back-pedal on a proposal to send Mexican troops as well.

The PRI's control of the legislature guaranteed NAFTA approval in Mexico, so the treaty's fate lay in the US Congress, which passed it by 34 votes in November 1993. Although nationalists were appalled at seeing Mexico's economic future being decided in Washington, NAFTA merely normalizes the facts of economic life, since 90 percent of Mexico's exports are to the US and 70 percent of its imports come from "the Other Side."

Mexico has many attractions: among the lowest wages in industrialized Latin America (Argentina, Chile, Brazil, Colombia, Venezuela, and Costa Rica all do better) and the buying power of some 30 million middle- or upper-class Mexicans, eager to consume US and Canadian goods. The treaty, which took force on 1 January 1994, seemed destined to join Mexico's economic future to the US economy for the foreseeable future.

Since NAFTA was signed, Mexico has risen from being the United States' fourth-largest to its second-largest trading partner – and may eclipse Canada for the number one spot within the next decade, if bilateral trade continues its post-NAFTA growth rate of twenty percent a year. Mexico now has free trade agreements with 29 other countries, including one with the fifteen-member European Union – making it the only country in the world, apart from Israel, to have free trade with the two biggest trading blocs.

NAFTA's first year was dogged by turbulence in Mexico, including the Zapatista revolt (timed to coincide with the treaty's inauguration) and a

Shoe-shiners and laptops – rich and poor meet at a sidewalk café in the fashionable La Condesa district of Mexico City

(L. Addario/ Network Photographers)

collapse of the peso after a bungled devaluation, sending the economy into deep recession and causing a banking crisis that would require a multi-billion dollar rescue organized by President Bill Clinton over the objections of the US Congress.

Under President Ernesto Zedillo, a dry and bookish technocrat, the economy rebounded to grow at 5.5 percent a year, foreign investors built new factories rather than sink cash into volatile short-term bonds (one of the main factors in the peso crash) and the country's finances improved to such an extent that it earned a coveted investment-grade rating from Moody's credit-risk agency. He left office with a 70 percent approval rating and a place in the history books for overseeing the transition to democracy.

As the benefits of NAFTA for Mexico become manifest – foreign investment of $10–12 billion a year, booming trade and job growth – opposition to the treaty has become increasingly muted. The one political party that still runs on a stridently anti-free trade platform, the leftist PRD, has suffered grievously at the polls.

Still, the benefits of NAFTA have been unevenly spread, with the export sector reaping the greatest advantages. It has done little for small- and medium-sized companies employing 90 percent of the workforce, which remain starved for credit thanks to continuing malaise in the banking sector. It has also exacerbated the country's geographical divide, in which the prosperous north – with its factories and giant export-oriented farms – has pulled even further ahead of the rural, impoverished south.

Even though former US President Bill Clinton insisted upon other agreements containing labor and environmental safeguards, NAFTA itself includes no social charter that makes respect for human rights a requirement for membership (as does the European Union charter). Nor does it permit workers to move across national borders within NAFTA, a problem that persistently aggravates bilateral relations.

President Fox has floated pet projects for a deepening of the free trade area into a genuine common market, with a development bank and free movement of workers across borders. But while the new US president, George W. Bush, has shown sympathy for Mexico's immigration concerns – and will likely approve some form of expanded guest worker program for Mexicans – a European Union-style arrangement remains an unrealistic prospect while the disparity in wealth between the two nations remains so great.

Engines of the Economy

The engines of the Mexican economy are energy production, export manufacturing, banking and finance, tourism, agriculture, and the informal sector (including the drug trade with the US).

A female worker in a maquiladora has a clothing assembly quality check.

(Chris Sharpe/ South American Pictures

Oil production remains at the hub of the economy. About half the daily output of three million barrels is destined for export, nearly 80 percent of it to the US. Whereas it once dominated exports, oil now accounts for a diminishing, though significant, share of the country's foreign revenues. But Pemex, the world's fifth largest oil corporation, has not kept pace with the industry and the oil sector's continuing strength is endangered by underinvestment – the company is used as a cash-cow by the government, to which it pays out two-thirds of its revenues in taxes.

Although Washington lobbied for Pemex privatization under NAFTA, Mexico resisted. Privatizing the industry is a political hot potato that requires constitutional amendment and could precipitate a nationalist backlash. Even Vicente Fox, who floated the idea early in his election campaign, has had to settle for merely reorganizing the company to put it on a more competitive footing. But even that is formidable challenge for an inefficient behemoth with 130,000 workers and a history of corruption and environmental neglect.

Oil production falls under the aegis of the Energy Secretariat, which also oversees the Federal Electricity Commission (CFE), responsible for generating 90 percent of the nation's electricity. The country's electricity industry faces an imminent shortage of both generating capacity and natural gas to supply it. To keep up with surging demand, Mexico must double gas production within seven years, as well as build a raft of new gas-fired generating stations, according to George Baker, director of Mexico Energy Intelligence, an industry newsletter in Houston. It's estimated that in order to do so, $25 billion will need to be invested in the electricity sector over the next decade, and another $50 in natural gas exploration and production – impossible sums for a country with an annual budget of only $120 billion.

Pemex has an emergency program for expanding gas drilling, but it seems likely that its efforts will fall far short. The alternative favored by the Fox government – abolishing Pemex's monopoly on gas production, and opening it and the electricity sector to foreign investment – will require amending the constitution. With nationalists in Congress bitterly opposed, it will be a formidable task.

The *maquiladora* industry of mostly border-based, foreign-owned assembly plants (although Mexicans own 30 percent of the facilities), is the largest export earner. In 1965 the maquiladoras were established to provide jobs for Mexicans returning from the curtailed *"bracero"* US guest-worker program. But even then, the "Maqs" were already seen as an American response to the offshore assembly operations of the Asian "Tigers." The industry took off after the 1982 devaluation of the peso reduced Mexican wages to the lowest of any first-tier Latin nation.

The first maquiladora operations involved simple tasks like sorting coupons. Today, the plants produce US defense system components. Some 3,700 maquiladora plants stretch along the northern border from Tijuana to Matamoros, employing 1.3 million workers. US corporations, often operating under other names, dominate production, with electrical assemblers like General Electric and Zenith running dozens of facilities. Japanese and Korean assemblers have moved into the maquila business, with a third of the industrial park space in Tijuana and Ciudad Juárez.

In pre-NAFTA times, US components were shipped across the border to be assembled and were then taxed a minimal amount for the value-added by labor (hence "maquila" or "toll-taker") before being sent back to the US. Maquila products were not available in Mexico and only a tiny proportion of Mexican materials were used in production. But the industry is busting out of the border enclaves in which the plants have been corralled for three decades and the definition of what constitutes a maquiladora is blurring.

The Mexican car industry, the beneficiary of $30 billion in new investment since NAFTA, has doubled its output in the past five years to 1.9 million vehicles and surpassed Canada and Japan as a supplier of auto-parts to the US market. Four-fifths of the output is exported to the US.

The sector, which has existed in Mexico since the 1950s, depends on a string of engine assembly plants in the northern states of Chihuahua and Coahuila (dubbed "Little Detroit"). General Motors has over fifty plants in

Mexico, producing everything from engine parts to whole cars. Ford, with high-tech facilities in Hermosillo, Sonora, has transferred whole lines to Mexico. DaimlerChrysler makes its popular PT Cruiser exclusively in Toluca, just outside Mexico City, alongside GM, Nissan, BMW, Volvo, and Mercedes. Volkswagen Mexico is the only producer in the world of both the new and old "Beetle" at its giant plant in central city of Puebla, and is the state's single largest exporter. Auto workers are better trained and paid (wages of up to $600 a month, versus $200 for maquiladora employees), and the growth of local suppliers means that the economic benefits are spread more widely.

Foreign investment has started to flow into other sectors, too. Guadalajara has become a major center for computer manufacturing, with companies like Flextronics, IBM, Hewlett-Packard, and Xerox flocking to the city's home state of Jalisco. Mobile phone giants Motorola and Nokia have facilities in Puebla. Mexico now produces 98 percent of all North American televisions.

The banking and finance sector, a driving force during the Salinas years, was badly bruised by the 1995 economic crisis. In 1991, then-President Salinas reprivatized eighteen banks and deregulated the industry. The banking industry nearly collapsed during the 1994 peso crisis, and a public bailout of insolvent banks will eventually cost Mexican taxpayers $100 billion – equivalent to one-fifth of GDP. Eventually, most would be sold off to foreign banks, among them Inverlat to Canada's Scotiabank; Serfin to Santander of Spain; Bancomer to BBVA; and Banamex to Citigroup. By mid-2001, it was estimated that some 80 percent of Mexican banking assets were in foreign hands.

Even today, Mexican banks are still reluctant to lend, preferring to make their money on treasury bills and short-term commercial paper. As a result, most Mexicans have no access to bank loans or any other form of official credit. Instead, they resort to informal neighborhood savings schemes known as *tanda*, in which a group of people pool their savings over a period of time and draw lots to take turns withdrawing money. This practice is institutionalized in companies specializing in *autofin* (self-financing); they are licensed by the government to facilitate purchases of new homes and cars.

Tourism is the third source of foreign currency (remittances from Mexicans working in the US are the fourth). Mexico claims seven million tourist visits a year, almost all from the US. Often, vacationers are flown pre-paid into Pacific and Caribbean enclaves, housed by transnational hotel chains, and have no contact with the real Mexico. Yet that reality is never very far away – fifteen tourist "mega-development" projects have sparked the growth of nearby squatter cities of the rural poor, lured in by the promise of work as day-laborers and maids. Mega-developments are sometimes built on beach land expropriated from local native peoples and their construction, although touted as ecologically sound because tourism is an industry "without smokestacks," threaten delicate tropical environments.

The informal sector combines licit and illicit commerce, the common bond being the inability of the Mexican government to collect taxes on transactions. Quantifying the informal sector is difficult – one College of Mexico study estimates between 25 and 38 percent of Mexico's economic output is generated by the informal sector, which provides jobs to a quarter of the nation's economically active population.

Mexico's cities are occupied by armies of street vendors. The invasion is timeless: mock-ups of Tenochtitlán at the National Anthropology Museum show *ambulantes* hawking their wares where the *zócalo* now stands. Selling on the street is big business. *Ambulantes* are organized into territorial groups that battle each other for sites and licenses and promise their votes to political parties, traditionally the PRI, in exchange for protection. If Mexican streets are straining at the seams with sellers, it is because the formal sector cannot provide nearly enough jobs. The economy has to grow at seven percent just to provide employment for the million young people entering the market each year.

Despite its shadowy origins, the underground economy is as socially stratified as the formal one. At the bottom are the urchins hawking *chicles* (chewing gum) at the traffic lights. Mid-level *micro-impresarios* cut hair in off-the-books shops. The kings of *fayuca* (contraband merchandise smuggled in by the trailer load) rule the streets of the tough inner-city Tepito neighborhood.

But the true kings of the informal sector are Mexico's drug lords, who earn anywhere from $5 billion to $30 billion a year from the narcotics trade with the United States. The production and movement of drugs is controlled by fourteen regionally based cartels that have penetrated deeply into police structures. Among the most notorious and violent is the Tijuana-based cartel of the Arellano Felix brothers.

Drug production in Mexico began in the Culiacán Valley of Sinaloa during the World War II when US pharmaceutical manufacturers, denied opium from the Far East for morphine production, contracted local farmers to sow legal poppy plantations. When the transnationals retired, they left behind a trained corps of *gomeros* who produced brown and black tar heroin for US southwest consumption. Combined with traditional marijuana production in the "Golden Triangle" of Durango, Chihuahua, and Sinaloa, the heroin routes north converted enterprising farm boys into powerful drug barons. When, in the early 1980s, Colombian cartels, deprived of Caribbean routes by increased US enforcement, moved transshipment operations to Mexico, the Sinaloa mafias were contracted to get the drugs into the US, and eventually became partners in the trade. Seventy percent of all cocaine now reaching the US market enters via Mexico, according to the DEA.

Drug lords such as Rafael Caro Quintero and the late Amado Carillo are legends with their own *corridos* (ballads) celebrating their exploits. But these men crave legitimacy, investing profits in legal businesses such as construction and the hotel industry. As the importance of drug-money in the economy grows, so does the political influence of the drug lords and corruption of government officials is now thought to rival Colombia.

5.   ART AND CULTURE

High and Low Art

On the Day of the Dead (November 2), many Mexican families create ingenious home altars, filled with mementos of the departed, garlands of Cempachutl (marigolds), stenciled paper (*papel picado*), delicately-molded skulls of spun sugar and traditional drinks and foods such as turkey *mole*. Day of the Dead altars are now exhibited in museums worldwide and collected by connoisseurs of folk art, but celebrating the *día de los muertos* also invokes living Nahua ritual, renewed from year to year as millions of Mexicans travel out to the tombs of their relatives for the traditional graveside feast.

The Day of the Dead pageant blends high art and "popular" culture in a uniquely Mexican fashion. Populism in Mexican art is a strand that has survived from the revolution. The most renowned Mexican painter of the century, Diego Rivera, saw his monumental murals as popular art, illustrating history for the unlettered masses. Today, his work, and that of his folk-art enthusiast wife, Frida Kahlo, is feverishly sought by collectors, with paintings fetching millions of dollars.

High art receives its stamp of approval from the government's Institute of Fine Arts. The art deco *Bellas Artes* palace adjoining Mexico City's historic center displays heroic murals by Rivera, David Alfaro Siquieros, José Clemente Orozco, and the apolitical Rufino Tamayo, whose earthy colors reflect his Oaxaca origin. *Bellas Artes* is also home to the *Ballet Folklórico de México*.

The "highness" of art is tested by the market place. In addition to 20th-century masters, colonial art is collected by Mexico's wealthiest families. A black market in colonial church artifacts thrives, as does the trade in pre-Colombian pieces. Under Mexican law, such works belong to the nation and should be held by the National Institute of Anthropology and History (INAH).

High art is financed by a generous system of state subsidies that pays for prizes, exhibitions, publishing contracts, artists and writers' grants, and scholarships to study abroad. Very often, these are controlled and dispensed by "mafias" or cliques of important writers, artists, and intellectuals. The late Mexican poet Octavio Paz, who died in 1998, was one such "cultural *caudillo*" (boss), whose entourage was based around the now-defunct literary journal *Vuelta*. Paz was the quintessential example of the Mexican intellectual-as-public figure – speaking out regularly on politics and policy, his opinions sought by presidents and cabinet ministers, his omnivorous interests ranging from birth control to religion to electoral reform. His resignation, in 1968, from his post as Mexican ambassador to India to protest the Tlatelolco massacre sowed the seeds of a culture of intellectual dissidence that inspired a generation of independent journalists and writers. But this tradition of the European-style "public intellectual" is on the decline in today's pluralistic Mexico. Indeed, there are few surviving writers of Paz's stature to keep up the tradition. His protégé, the historian Enrique Krauze, is one of the few. Krauze's literary and current affairs magazine *Letras Libres* is widely respected – as is his documentary series on Mexican history and society, *Mexico Nuevo Siglo*. The novelist Carlos Fuentes is another, although his influence is limited by the fact that he divides his time between Mexico and abroad.

Culture in Mexico has traditionally been shaped and guided by state institutions, and that is as true today as it was in the years after the Revolution, when the country's new leaders set out to create public art that would legitimize and glorify their rule – like the murals of Diego Rivera.

At the federal level, cultural subsidies flow through such bodies as the National Council on Culture and the Arts (Conaculta), the National Culture Fund (Fonca), the Fine Arts Institute (Bellas Artes) and the state-run foundation Fondo de Cultura Económica, a publishing house that is the largest in Latin America.

At the local level, the number of funding agencies is diverse: city, state, and local governments, as well most large universities, each have their own departments of *difusión cultural* (cultural dissemination). The most

Costume parade on the Day of the Dead,.Oaxaca

(Robert Francis/ South American Pictures

important of these belong to the National Autonomous University of Mexico (UNAM) and the Mexico City government.

Increasingly, private groups like the Fundación Pascual have joined the scene, and coupled with the growing independence of the Mexican media, the grip of the old "mafias" of high culture has loosened somewhat.

Urban Pop Culture

Popular culture gets its stamp of approval from the mass audiences it attracts, mainly drawn from the *clase popular* (working class). A top-selling album of *corridos* (ballads) or ranchero music (comparable to US country & western) can sell millions of CDs. By contrast, a literary novel by an established local author will have a print run of no more than 5,000 copies.

The most popular literary form is the *historieta*, the distinctive pocket-sized comic books that are devoured in their hundreds of thousands by working-class readers. Millions of Mexicans learned to read from *historietas*, which were often used in government literacy campaigns. At its peak in the early 1980s, the Mexican comic book industry had a readership of as many as 26 million people – more than a third of the population at the time.

Grotesque, garish, obscene, violent, and often outrageously sentimental, today's *historietas* reveal in barely inhibited form the dark underside of the

Historietas – narrative comics – are the most popular literary form in Mexico.

(Editorial Mango)

national psyche. Women are invariably depicted as buxom, sex-starved, Scandinavian-style beauties; men are often portrayed as buffoons, betrayed by their *machismo*, brutality, and fecklessness. Intrigue, betrayal, sexual crime, detective, and cowboy stories, the sanctity of the family and the Virgin – these are the staples of the *historieta* world.

Lucha libre (professional wrestling) was originally an American import in the 1930s. But Mexican culture has left a deep imprint on the sport and made it one of the country's favorite forms of entertainment. Its popularity is epitomized by the career of the late Rodolfo Guzman, who became known to millions as *El Santo* (The Saint). Super-hero, matinee idol, and man of mystery (he never took off his distinctive silver mask in public), he starred in comic books and dozens of B-movies with titles like "Santo versus Dracula" and "Santo in the House of Death."

The Mexican wrestler's use of a mask to conceal his identity recalls the costumes of Aztec warriors and Christian Saints, and serves as a metaphor for a Mexico that conceals its true face from the outside world. Visiting American wrestlers are almost always given the role of *rudos* (villains) and are invariably thrashed by their Mexican opponents in symbolic revenge for a history of national humiliation by gringos. But by far the most popular foreign wrestler of the last decade was Ian Hodgkinson, a former bouncer from Thunder Bay, Ontario, who fought under stage name *El Vampiro Canadiense* (the Canadian vampire).

Television is the most powerful medium of mass culture in Mexico, and the most popular genre on TV is the *telenovela* (soap opera). These Latin melodramas are mass-produced by both of Mexico's main national broadcasters, Televisa and TV Azteca. Unlike their American cousins, *telenovelas* last only a single season – usually six months – based on a story structure with a beginning, middle, and end.

Mexican prime time – loosely defined as 4 PM to 10 PM – is programmed wall-to-wall with *telenovelas*, each one fine-tuned to appeal to a specific demographic: children, teenagers, housewives, educated professionals, and families. Most who watch, though, are working-class Mexicans for whom the escapist Cinderella fantasy offered by *telenovelas* is an antidote the boredom and hopelessness of their daily life.

It's hard to understate the central importance of the *telenovela* in Mexican popular culture. With audiences of up to 25 million people for a hit *novela*, they bring in the lion's share of revenues for broadcasters. *Telenovela* actors are at the center of the Mexican "star system," in which music, films, theater, magazine publishing, and multi-media are linked in a seamless web of cross-promotions. The telenovela is Mexico's Hollywood, and the nexus of its culture of celebrity.

Dancing is also an integral part of Mexican popular culture. From an early age, children are taught social dances such as *cumbia, merengue*, and *salsa* at family fiestas. As adults, they may practice them at an old-fashioned *salon de baile* (dance hall) or the more contemporary *antro* (dance club). Most big Mexican cities are dotted with dance schools, teaching everything from cha-cha-cha to American-style jive, and many restaurants have live bands and dance floors.

The films of the beloved scamp Cantinflas are another beacon of Mexican popular art. Even the most sophisticated Mexican movie stars in an industry that peaked in the 1940s and 1950s, such as the glamorous María Félix and Pedro Infante, portrayed singing cowboys and simple peasants. In the process, they turned the figure of the *mariachi* musician into a living icon of Mexican culture, who can still be found today in Mexico City's Plaza Garibaldi, gathering in their scores to be hired to play for *fiestas* or romantic serenades.

According to Professor Anne Rubenstein of Toronto's York University, Mexicans began referring to the growing number of B-movies produced after the 1950s as *churros*, a reference to the machine-made crullers sold on every street corner – sweet and enjoyable, but easily forgettable and certainly not nourishing. There were movies based on fashionable dances, like the *cha-cha-cha*; on popular characters like the lady truck-driver *Lola la trailera* and *La India Maria* (Maria the Indian), a wise innocent who gives slick city-dwellers their comeuppance; and on comic-book characters like *Kaliman, el hombre increible* (Kaliman, the incredible man).

Mexican cinema went into decline in the 70s and 80s, churning out exploitation films that drove away the middle-class Mexican audiences that had earlier patronized the cinema. Movie theaters fell into disuse – with ticket prices frozen at artificially low levels, owners had no incentive to maintain them or build new ones. Later, under President Carlos Salinas, ticket prices were freed and chains of American-style megaplexes sprang up around the country.

The film production industry began to revive again in the final decade of the 20th century, partly fueled by an influx of Hollywood productions taking advantage of the low cost of shooting in Mexico, like *Titanic* and Baz Lurhmann's remake of *Romeo + Juliet*.

A new generation of Mexican directors was also coming of age. With the aid of the governmental Mexican Institute of Cinematography (Imcine), they began making films that put Mexico back on the map of independent cinema. With features like *Santitos* (Little Saints), the biting political satire *La Ley de Herodes* (Herod's Law), the bedroom comedy *Sexo, pudor y lagrimas* (Sex, Shame, and Tears) and the critically acclaimed *Amores Perros* (Savage Love), the Mexican film industry showed that it could lure middle-class audiences back into the theaters with smart and sophisticated products that could compete strongly against Hollywood.

The clash of the fine and the popular touches every aspect of Mexican art. The most critically acclaimed photographers, like Manuel Alvarez Bravo or Nacho López, compose elegant portraits of the country's vibrant street life. Even the art of Mexican cuisine echoes its popular roots. Nopal cactus pods and chocolate-dusted *moles,* foods of the Mexican rural poor, are now featured on world-class menus. Laura Esquivel's book and film, *Like Water for Chocolate,* extols the glories of Mexico's kitchens.

The National Museum of Anthropology is the apogee of Mexico's fascination with the past, but the magnificent relics displayed portray a dead and archived version of indigenous cultures that are still intensely alive. Nurtured and enriched as their art passes from generation to generation, the Nahua Day of the Dead altars, the brilliant textiles of the Maya, the pottery of the Purépechas, the band music of the Mijes, and the Holy Week dances of the Raramuri may, indeed, be Mexico's highest, and most durable, art.

The Word

In the beginning, there were the Mexica and Maya codices, complex series of pictographs bound into books that illustrated every aspect of their civilizations. Most were destroyed by Spanish moralists such as Bishop Landa of Mérida, who called the books the work of Satan and piled the priceless codices onto the bonfires of the Inquisition in 1556. Saved from the flames were the Popul Vuh and the Chilam Balam, prophetic Mayan texts that preserved the oral tradition.

Farther north, in the Valley of Mexico, Nezahualcoyotl, the poet lord of Texcoco, provides a strong voice from the pre-European past. His verses, lovingly translated by Miguel León-Portillo, are the oldest surviving fragments of pre-Columbian poetry.

The first significant poet to emerge after the Conquest was Sor Juana Ines de la Cruz (1651–95), a nun who wrote sexy, passionate poetry still considered among the best in 17th-century Spanish literature.

Mexican poetry, like the plastic arts, reflects both the high and the popular. Street poets cadge coins by reciting verses in Mexico City subway cars, and the Huapango music of eastern Mexico features contests between quick-tongued versifiers. At the highbrow end of the spectrum, Mexico's Nobel laureate Octavio Paz's limpid, precise lines are some of the most luminous of the 20th century.

Mexico City boasts a lively literary scene, matched in the Americas only by Buenos Aires, with nightly presentations at venues like the San Angel Cultural Center and a huge annual book fair – a cultural irony in a country where illiteracy remains unconquered.

Octavio Paz,
who died in 1998
(Julio Etchart/ Reportage)

Neither Paz nor the more experimental Carlos Fuentes is considered the finest prose writers of their day. That honor goes to magic realist Juan Rulfo who before his death in 1986 completed *Pedro Páramo*, a ghostly tale of death and loss set in an abandoned Jalisco dreamscape, and a key Mexican contribution to the literary "Latin Boom." Paz, whose *Labyrinth of Solitude* (1952) probed the Mexican psyche, was the patriarch of the nation's *belles lettres*. The oft-expatriate Fuentes, influenced by the US writer William Faulkner, is politically adventurous and dubbed "the guerrilla dandy" by conservative historian Enrique Krauze.

Younger Mexican writers have felt less drawn to the themes of history, folklore, and nation building that inspired earlier generations. Jorge Volpi, one of the most admired young writers in Mexico today, gained literary stardom in the late 1990s with *En Busca de Klingsor* (In Search of Klingsor), a novel about Germany and the development of the atomic bomb. Ignacio Padilla, Juan Villoro, and Daniel Sada are also identified with this new, more cosmopolitan literary trend.

Today's most read non-fiction prose writers are Carlos Monsiváis, an urbane chronicler of Mexican society; Elena Poniatowska, whose documentary collages give a voice to the voiceless; and Paco Ignacio Taibo II, a left-wing writer of *policiacas* (detective stories). All three write for *La Jornada*, a fifteen-year-old left-wing independent national daily.

The word is communicated via Mexico's corner news kiosks. In Mexico City alone, nearly 30 papers appear daily and some provincial cities produce a dozen more.

During PRI rule, there was no overt censorship of the press but the government had a multitude of subtler ways to control what was went into print. The main levers of control were financial. Most newspapers subsisted on government advertising and the *sobres* (envelopes of money), routinely passed to reporters in return for glorifying a political or business leader. *Gacetillas*, or paid political articles, were run as straight news stories portraying their sponsors in a flattering light. Journalists were allowed to sell advertising on commission. The government kept publishers in line by controlling the supply of newsprint. Newspaper kiosks, run by a union loyal to the PRI, would refuse to sell publications deemed hostile to the government.

The 1990s saw a gradual loosening of controls on the media, as newspapers and journalists became increasingly independent. The leading paper of Mexico's democratic era is *Reforma*, part of a media empire that includes *El Norte* of Monterrey and *Mural* of Guadalajara. With its investigative reporting and arms-length relationship from power, the company has incurred the wrath of PRI presidents from Jose Lopez Portillo to Ernesto Zedillo. At one point in 1982, publisher Alejandro Junco de la Vega had to flee with his family to Texas after running a headline critical of the head of state.

Journalists on the paper – among the youngest and best paid in the business – are barred from accepting bribes or selling advertising, most of which comes from the private sector. The company had to create its own distribution system from scratch after the kiosks refused to carry it. It created its own independent polling unit, and its monthly opinion polls are among the most reliable indicators of public sentiment in the country.

Despite the number of papers, readership is minuscule compared to the US and Europe – total newspaper readership is barely 1 million. *La Prensa*, a lurid daily that specializes in the *nota roja* (crime stories), is the nation's best-selling newspaper, claiming 400,000 circulation. The O'Farrell family publishes two national newspapers (including the English-language *News*) and dominates the magazine racks, producing everything from *historietas* to the Mexican edition of *Vogue*.

Enrique Krauze's slickly designed *Letras Libres*, the high-minded *Nexos*, the popular and readable *Milenio*, and the insightful *Proceso*, a financially struggling investigative newsweekly with no government advertising, are Mexico's most prestigious magazines. But the crucial media for communications in Mexico is electronic. Television and radio are the nation's primary source of news and information about itself. Millions of Mexicans listen to talk radio, with its flamboyant on-air personalities, raunchy language of *albur* (sexual double-entendres), and practical jokes competing in outrageousness.

The TV airwaves are dominated by the giant Televisa Corporation, which claims 40 million viewers, running four out of the five national networks and hundreds of repeater stations. The corporation was founded in 1948 by the late Emilio Azcárraga, a fervent supporter of the PRI whose loyalty was rewarded with lucrative broadcast monopolies. Televisa was one of the main pillars of PRI rule, supplying an endless flow of sympathetic news coverage of government policies while ignoring or excoriating its opponents. But with the ouster of the old ruling party, the giant broadcaster has become increasingly fair and balanced in its coverage.

Televisa's main competitor is TV Azteca, a formerly state-owned network that was privatized in the mid-1990s. The upstart network made a name for itself with sophisticated, realistic telenovelas that dealt with previously taboo subjects – like *Nada Personal* (Nothing Personal), which starkly depicted official corruption and links to drug traffickers; and *Mirada de Mujer* (A Woman's Gaze), which dealt with adultery and female sexuality. In the process, it attracted educated, middle-class audiences to a genre that had largely been the domain of working-class viewers.

Rock music was an early Anglo-American cultural import and had an immediately powerful influence. The earliest Mexican groups not only sang in English, in imitation of their idols like The Beatles and The Doors, but gave themselves English names – like *Three Souls on my Mind*, one of the few bands of that period that still survives today, though renamed as *El Tri*.

But rock music was anathema to the Mexican establishment. The left saw it as cultural imperialism, while the right regarded it as a menace to moral values, tradition, and the family. The official musicians' union didn't like the competition, and the government was wary of any cultural expression it couldn't manipulate for its own political ends. A public bonfire of Elvis records in the *zócalo* in the late 50s was symptomatic of the official attitude.

These anti-rock forces came together in September 1971, when the Avándaro music festival – a Mexican version of Woodstock that was the first of its kind in Latin America – was shut down by the authorities. This was the start of a campaign of official suppression of rock that would last for more than a decade, in which bands were forced underground, playing in so-called *hoyos funkis* (literally, funky holes) – generally rented warehouses. Prior to the Salinas economic liberalization, even Mexican-born rock idol Carlos Santana was barred from appearing in the capital. But by the late 1980s, bands were again playing openly and new groups were being formed, like *Maldita Vecindad, Santa Sabina,* and *Caifanes* (now known as *Jaguares*). Radio stations, which had once shunned Spanish-language rock, embraced the concept of *rock en tu idioma* (rock in your own language) and began giving airtime to Mexican bands. The big transnational record companies gave their seal of approval to the new music by signing *rock en español* bands en masse. Groups like *Café Tacuba* and singer-songwriter Julieta Venegas have large followings outside

Mexico, where their fusion of Mexican folk traditions and modern rock has created a distinctive sound.

But Mexican rock retains its raw and anti-authoritarian edge, and no commemoration of the Tlatelolco massacre or Zapatistas fundraiser takes place without a concert. The spiritual home of Mexican rock can found at *El Chopo*, an open-air swap meet and rock-and-roll paraphernalia market that takes place every Saturday near the abandoned Buenavista railway station in central Mexico City.

"So Close to the United States..."

Two thousand miles of border reminds the United States of Mexico just how lengthy its relationship with the United States of America has been. The shadow of the US casts itself over every facet of Mexican life – from the American fast-food outlets and giant retailers that dot the landscape, to the hip-hop music that blares from countless radios, to the Hollywood films that dominate the megaplexes, to the subtle and not-so-subtle pressures that Washington exerts on every issue of national importance. Mexicans resent being told what to do by outsiders – even daylight savings time is seen by many as an unwarranted foreign imposition.

The love-hate relationship between Mexico and the United States has roots in the 1848 Treaty of Guadalupe Hidalgo and the repeated incursions of gringo troops onto Mexican soil. Conversely, both Mexico's independence struggle and its 1910 Revolution drew inspiration from the ideals of the American Revolution. Indeed, the country's official name is the United States of Mexico – a measure of its aspirations to absorb what is best of the American experience.

Gazing up their northern neighbor, many Mexicans envy the prosperity of its economy, the efficiency and honesty of its bureaucracy, the tolerance and freedom of its citizens, and the boundless energy of its people. But they also worry about the survival of their own culture. Mexico is a predominantly young country (half the population has not yet reached its 25th birthday) and the fads, foods, and fashions that pour south from the US make the old ways seem irrelevant. The forces of globalization have given this process fresh momentum.

But at the same, time they have opened new spaces for the reverse flow: a blossoming of Mexican culture that crosses the Rio Grande. Mexican films, TV, music, Internet content, and multimedia are reaching audiences in the United States as never before. The 20.6 million Mexican-American diaspora in the United States – already the largest single ethnic group in California, Texas, and other states of the Southwest – is growing politically and culturally assertive, with Spanish emerging as that country's unofficial second language.

Fears that Mexican culture will be submerged by a wave of Americanization are almost certainly exaggerated. Mexican civilization spans three millennia and has just begun a fourth. Thus far, it has always managed to resist and absorb all other cultural invasions from the north. The clash of a brash young US consumer culture and a Mexico so heavily weighted by the past will leave a profound mark upon this nation for generations to come.

WHERE TO GO, WHAT TO SEE

For those who enter Mexico by land, travelling across the northern border, the transition can be particularly abrupt – it is often said that this is the only land border between the 'first' and 'third' worlds on the planet. The shortest route runs from Matamoros on the Gulf to Mexico City in just under 24 hours. But the journey is just as scenic south from Nuevo Laredo or Ciudad Juárez thorough the Chihuahua desert, and can be downright dangerous down the Pacific coast (trainwrecks, *bandidos* and bad cops) from Nogales.

Moving by bus (reserve window seats, stay away from the TV screens that have now invaded almost all fleets) and train (more problematic), you will get to know two worlds, the one outside and the one within. The conviviality of long-haul passengers is legendary – you will meet folks who you will remember for a lifetime (take names and numbers and add them to your Mexico network). Besides the spectacular scenery, you'll eat native foods (try goat stew *birria* in San Luis Potosí), learn amazing new slang, and explore the social and political landscape through which you are passing (buy newspapers for clues).

Eventually you will arrive in Mexico City, and with luck and eternal vigilance, you may even have all your luggage. If history is your cup of tea, the *Centro Histórico* will satiate. All sorts of hotels, from extreme luxury to seedy fleabag, line the streets spoking off from the great, flat zócalo square. Settle in, expanding your radius block by blocks – let the Metro and your own feet propel you around the city.

The Museum of the Temple of the Plaza Mayor, on the northeast corner of the zócalo, is a better starting point for finding the ancients than the gargantuan Anthropological museum out in Chapultepec Park. Once outside, head north down Argentina street until you hit the thieves' market of Tepito (hold onto your wallet), then veer due south towards La Merced, the grandest produce market in all Latin America.

Mexico City radiates power from intriguing points: the pyramid of the sun at Teotihuacán (buses from the Indios Verdes metro) and *Los Pinos*, the Presidential mansion on the Constituyentes edge of the park (strictly off-limits); the *Palacio Legislativo* or Mexican Chamber of Deputies east of La Merced, the National Palace fronting the zócalo (with the famous Rivera murals). Other sites of light and darkness – Tepeyac Hill, where the Virgin of Guadalupe engineered the first 'Mexican Miracle' in La Villa at the north end of the city; the floating gardens of Xochimilco on the extreme south; the *Panteón Dolores*, the sprawling cemetery in the west of Chapultepec

The El Castillo pyramid at Chichén Itzá. *(Michiel Dethmers)*

(particularly around the Day of the Dead, 1-2 November, although the best pageantry is found at Misquic in the Tlahuac delegation).

To see more of colonial Mexico, make a side trip to Morelia, six hours outside of Mexico City in the state of Michoacán. More spectacularly, arrive in late October or early November to see the millions of migrating monarch butterflies that carpet the El Rosario Monarch Butterfly Sanctuary, just a few hours outside of Morelia.

Push south through the Cuatla valley of Morelos and sign the guest book at the house and Museum of Emiliano Zapata at Anenecuilco. Catch a slow train towards Puebla past the volcanoes. Or else head for *tierra caliente* through Guerrero, putting in perhaps at Iztcateopan (near Taxco) where the bones of the Emperor Cuauhtémoc are displayed under the altar in the town church (priests hid them for centuries). Zigzag down the 'Costa Chica' south of Acapulco into the Afro zone on both sides of the Oaxaca-Guerrero border.

Don't forget to stop in Oaxaca, with its stately multi-coloured colonial architecture that will take you back to the 16th century. As one of the centers of indigenous culture, this is a good place to wander the busy markets, listening to the mix of ancient languages and looking for local crafts and the painted *animalitos* carved from wood. If you have a strong stomach, you can also try the local specialty, *chapulines*, or fried grasshoppers. For the less courageous, there are the delicious soups of *flor de calabaza; quesillo*, a salty Oaxacan string cheese; and endless varieties of *mole* to choose from. From Oaxaca it is only 101 km to the Tlacolula Valley, where Mixtec and Zapotec culture thrived since their origins in the 7th century BC. The breathtaking Zapotec site of Monte Albán, set into a high plateau encircled by the surrounding mountains, is not to be missed. Similarly a visit to Mitla, where stonework from the destroyed temples was used to build the colonial church of San Pablo, and the tiny villages located throughout the valley offer a rare view into an ancient way of life.

Jump on a bus and head for the Oaxacan Pacific Coast, where there are still small fishing towns and unspoilt beaches to explore. Sleep in *palapas* (palmfrond shelters) along the white beaches all the way to Tehuantepec. Beachfront villages like Puerto Angel, Zipolite, Ventanilla, and Mazunte are still off the tourist track. Mazunte has turned to eco-tourism and is home to the Centro Mexicano de la Tortuga, a museum that conducts research and breeding in an attempt to save the turtle population. Also nearby is Laguna Manialtepec, a natural freshwater lagoon encircled by mangroves that is home to hundreds of bird and plant species.

For those of you who caught the train to Puebla, follow Cortés' track down to the Caribbean, noting the snow-capped peaks of Orizaba and Malinche to the left and right. Veraruz is still a working port – find Café de la Parroquia for the best *café-con-leche* in all Mexico. At dusk, couples move in time to the elegant, understated *danzón* as the sun sinks below the sea.

Both the Pacific and Caribbean routes will take you to the Maya, converging in the jewel box Chiapas highland city of San Cristóbal de las Casas. From there, it's not far to the Lacandón jungle and the site of the Zapatista rebellion (although authorities can be tough on foreigners who want to visit the autonomous communities; people are sometimes deported – seek the latest advice). Nearby are the sensational Maya ruins at Palenque. Continue northeast along the *Ruta de los Mayas*, carefully avoiding the myriad tourism traps. Uxmal is less crowded than Chichén Itzá. The walled pirate city of Campeche is off the beaten track. So is Motul, north of Mérida near the top of the Yucatán, where the Mayan past lives in language and culture.

In your travels, look always for what is lost or in danger of being lost: the old ways of doing things, disappearing species and forests and languages, the art and the dream. Never avoid a fiesta. Do not shy away from the obvious, the poverty and startling class divides, the corruption and the

Tulúm, a Maya city whose idyllic setting on the
Caribbean draws increasing numbers of visitors

(South American Pictures)

violence that breaks through the surface of Mexican society all too often.

Travel is a two-way trek. We carry much more home than we bring in our backpacks and our suitcases. Mexico will give you memories, epiphanies, smells, sensations and wisdom. You will always go back.

FURTHER READING

HISTORY

A Traveller's History of Mexico, by Kenneth Pearce, Interlink Publishing, New York and Northampton, MA, 2002

Mexico: Biography of Power, Enrique Krauze, translated by Hank Heifetz, 1997

The Discovery and Conquest of Mexico, Bernal Díaz del Castillo, New York, 1956

The Broken Spears: The Aztec Account of the Conquest of Mexico, Miguel Léon Portilla, Boston, 1962

Aztec and *Aztec Autumn,* two novels by Gary Jennings, New York, 1980 and 1998

La Capital: The Biography of Mexico City, Jonathan Kandall, New York, 1988

The Oxford History of Mexico, Michael C. Meyer, William H. Beezley (editors), August 2000

THE MEXICAN REVOLUTION

Zapata and the Mexican Revolution, John Womack, New York, 1969

Insurgent Mexico, John Reed, New York, 1969

Memoires of Pancho Villa, Martin Luis Guzmán, Austin, 1965

Barbarous Mexico, John Kenneth Turner, Austin, 1969

The Rebellion of the Hanged, Bruno Traven, one of four "Monteria" novels (Hill & Wang, 1936)

The Underdogs, a novel by Mariano Azuela, (University of Pittsburgh Press, 1992)

The Power and The Glory, a post-revolutionary novel by Graham Greene, London, 1969

CONTEMPORARY EVENTS AND SOCIOLOGY

True Tales from Another Mexico: The Lynch Mob, the Popsicle Kings, Chalino, and the Bronx, Sam Quinones, University of New Mexico Press, 2001

The Heart that Bleeds: Latin America Today, Alma Guillermoprieto, 1995

Looking for History: Dispatches from Latin America, Alma Guillermoprieto, 2001

The Labyrinth of Solitude, Octavio Paz , New York, 1962

The Children of Sánchez, Oscar Lewis, New York, 1961

Mexico: The Struggle for Peace and Bread, Frank Tannenbaum, New York, 1950

Distant Neighbors, Alan Riding, New York, 1985

Mexico: A Country Guide, Tom Barry (ed), Albuquerque, 1992

The Mexican Economy 1996, published annually in English by the Banco de Mexico, Mexico City

Limits to Friendship: Mexico and the United States, Jorge G. Castañeda and Robert Pastor, New York, 1988

Generals In the Palacio, Roderic Ai Camp, New York, 1992

Massacre In Mexico, Elena Poniatowska (translation of *Noches de Tlatelolco*), New York, 1975

Juan the Chamula, Ricardo Pozas, Berkeley CA, 1962

Rebellion From the Roots: Indian Uprising in Chiapas, John Ross, Maine, 1995

The War Against Oblivion: Zapatista Chronicles 1994-2000, John Ross, Common Courage Press

ART, LITERATURE AND POPULAR CULTURE

Mexico City: A Cultural and Literary Companion, by Nick Caistor, Interlink Publishing, New York and Northampton, MA, 2000

The Fabulous Life of Diego Rivera, Bertram Wolf, London, 1968

Pedro Páramo, a novel by Juan Rulfo, New York, 1959

The Death of Artemio Cruz, or any one of a dozen novels by Carlos Fuentes, London, 1964

The Dead Girls, a novel by Jorge Iberguengoita, London, 1981

Light From A Nearby Window, contemporary Mexican poetry edited by Juvenal Acosta, San Francisco, 1993

The Plumed Serpent, D.H. Lawrence, New York, 1951

Under the Volcano, Malcolm Lowry, New York, 1965

Bad Language, Naked Ladies and Other Threats to the Nation, a Political History of Comic Books in Mexico, Anne Rubenstein, Duke University Press, 1998

Refried Elvis: The Rise of Mexican Counterculture, Eric Zolov, University of California Press, 1999

SELECTED WEBLINKS

www.cnart.mx
—Consejo Nacional para la Cultura y las Artes. Up-to-date information on music, dance festivals, art, and literature in Mexico. In Spanish.

www.arts-history.mx
—Artes e Historia de Mexico, Foro Virtual de Cultura. In Spanish. A slightly over-complex website featuring a virtual guide to Mexico City, cinema reviews, bookshop, and links.

www.mayadiscovery.com
—Mundo Maya online; general, accessibly written information on the culture, history, and current life of Mexico and Central America's Maya peoples.

www.mexiconetwork.info
—a unique collaboration between three English-language content providers Mexico Connect, Mexicanwave, and Planeta, this portal focuses on tourism, education, and journalism resources.

planeta.com
—dedicated to Latin America with a special focus on environmental issues, this is the most useful site for ecotravel and general information about Mexico. Note the Mexico travel directory and the directory of Spanish language schools in the Mexico links.

www.mexicanwave.com
—well-maintained and colorful UK-based portal for all things Mexican. Buy paintings, pi atas, posters, and books; browse tours and flight operators' links, as well as background on Mexican culture and customs.

www.mexconnect.com
—Mexico-based, ex-pat community-focused website offering news, travel links, tips on living and retiring in Mexico or buy Tabasco sauce online.

www.mexico-travel.com
—run by the Mexican Ministry of Tourism, focussed on tourism-related statistics and official reports. In Spanish.

www.jornada.unam.mx
—left-of-center Mexican daily newspaper online. In Spanish.

flag.blackened.net/revolt/zapatista.html
—Zapatista portal, with timeline of the conflict, background, and further reading suggestions.

FACTS AND FIGURES

GEOGRAPHY

Official name: Estados Unidos de México

Situation: Northernmost Latin American republic, bordering on USA to the North (3,119 km long, from Tijuana marker #258 east to Gulf of Mexico), Guatemala and Belize to the Southeast. Between 14° 30' and 32° 30' N and 87° and 117° West. Coastlines on the Gulf of California and Pacific Ocean in the West and the Gulf of Mexico and Caribbean in the East. Total land area is 1,967,183 sq km (equal to France, Spain, Britain, Germany and Italy combined), making it the third largest Latin American country (after Brazil and Argentina), and the 14th largest nation in world (although much smaller than its NAFTA partners, the US (9,312,614 sq km) and Canada (9,976,129 sq km).

Administrative Structure: 31 states and the federal district (Mexico City), *Capital:* Mexico City, population 8.605.239 million (2000 census), but total population of metropolitan area is nearer 20 million. *Other principal cities:* Guadalajara (1.6 million), Nezahualcotl (part of Mexico City metropolitan area) (1.3 million), Monterrey (1.1 million), Puebla (1.1 million).

MEXICO

0   250 km

State Boundaries

1 AGUASCALIENTES
2 GUANAJUATO
3 QUERETARO
4 HIDALGO
5 MEXICO (Toluca)
6 DISTRITO FEDERAL (Mexico City)
7 TLAXCALA
8 PUEBLA
9 MORELOS

74 per cent of Mexicans live in cities.

Infrastructure: There are 307,142 km of roads (94,235 paved) over which travel 12 million registered vehicles (3.8 million in Federal District). Mexico has 26,443 km of railroad and 76 marine ports. There are 13.6 million telephones, of which 8.5 million are residential.

Relief and Landscape: Highest Peaks are Citlaltepetl (Orizaba, 5,610 meters), Popocatepetl (5,500m), Iztaccihuatl (5,200m), Toluca Nevada (4,680m); Matlalcueyatl (Malinche, 4,200). Mexico has 16 active volcanoes. The longest rivers are the Balsas (west, 771km), the Lerma (central Mexico, 551km), and the Grijalba (isthmus, 433km). A lake

system that includes Lakes Chapala (1,080 sq kms), Pátzcuaro, and Cuitzeo is centered in west-central Mexico. Forested land covers 66 million hectares, agricultural land accounts for 108,346,000 hectares in arable farms and cattle ranches. 28 per cent of the land is classified as 'dry' and 20.8 as 'very dry'. Tabasco (1,686 mm rainfall annually) and Chiapas (1,256 mm) are the wettest states in the Mexican union.

POPULATION

2000 census estimates the population at 97,483,412 million (11th in world); it counts 47,592,253 million men and 49,891,159 million women. 38.3 per cent of the population under 15 years old. The average family has 2.5 children. Population density is 45.6 per sq km; densest is the Federal District (5494 per sq km), lowest is Baja California Sur (4 per sq km). Fastest growing population is that of Mexico State (9.8 million) but Quintana Roo and Baja California Norte have also tripled their populations since 1970. National population growth rate is 1.9 per cent (1990-2000). Population distribution in Mexico is evenly divided between rural and urban. Thus, 25.4 per cent of Mexicans live in localities with 2,500 inhabitants or less, while 26.4 per cent live in cities with more than 500,000 residents. For the rest of the population, 13.7 per cent reside in semi-rural towns of 2,500 to 15,000 people; 13.6 per cent live in communities of 15,000 to 100,000 inhabitants; and 21.0 per cent live in cities of 100,000 to 500,000 residents.

Health: Life expectancy is 71.7 years (68.7 men, women 74.9). Infant mortality has dropped from 93 deaths per 1,000 live births in 1960 to

MEXICO

0 _____ 250 km

Climate and Natural Vegetation

Monterrey

Guadalajara

MEXICO CITY

▓ Tropical rainforest

▒ Savanna (short dry season)

░ Steppe (long dry season)

▫ Desert

▥ Temperate

▤ Subtropical

25.4 per 1,000 in 2000. But, in 1998 infant mortality among the richest 20 per cent was 13 per 1,000, whereas for the poorest 20 per cent it was 52 per 1,000, four times as high. Eight million children are considered malnourished. In 2000, Mexico registered 120.0 physicians, 191.1 nurses and 77.5 hospital beds per 100,000 people. Approximately 4,200 people died of HIV/AIDS in 1999.

Education: For 2000, the population aged 15 years and older registered an illiteracy rate of 9.5 per cent (men 7.4 per cent, women 11.3 per cent). In the same year, 92.3 per cent of the population aged 6 to 14 years attended school. Nevertheless, 28.2 per cent of the population aged

15 years and over remained without instruction and had not completed elementary school. The average schooling of the population aged 15 years and over was 7.6 years in 2000, as compared to 6.6 years in 1990. However, Mexico has a bigger schooling gap between rich and poor. In the mid-1990s the poorest 10% of its children averaged only 2.1 years; the richest 10%, 12.1 years.

Poverty Measures: 28.6 per cent Mexicans live in poverty and 8.2 per cent in 'extreme poverty' (6.1 per cent in 1980) according to World Bank 1996 calculations. The minimum wage for Mexico city is worth approximately US$4 a day, though

ECONOMIC INDICATORS AND TRADE

government statistics indicate a third of the working population earns less than that minimum. A World Bank report from 1996 said that one-fourth of Mexicans earned less than U.S.$2 a day and that 17 percent of Mexicans earned less than U.S.$1 a day.

Indigenous Peoples:
Indigenous people account for only 7.1 per cent of population over age 5 when language is the criteria (6,044,547 are classified as speaking an ethnic language in 2000). Of the ethnic speaking population, 24.0 per cent speak Náhuatl, 13.2 per cent speak Maya, 7.2 per cent speak Zapoteco, and 7.0 per cent speak Mixteco, with the remainder divided over various other languages.

Environment: Mexico is host to 449 species of mammals (2nd in world), 69 of which are endangered; 1150 species of birds (11th in world), 39 endangered; 717 species of reptiles (first in world), 18 endangered; and 281 species of amphibians (fourth in world), 4 endangered. Deforestation continues at a rapid rate, exceeding 600,000 hectares (1.5 million acres) a year, while annual reforestation is less than one-tenth of that figure.

2000 GDP – US$ 574.5 billion (GDP per capita – US$5,810). GDP average annual growth rate (2000) 4.3 per cent, but was a provisional -[minus]7.0 per cent in 1995. GDP composition by sector was 4.4 per cent agriculture, 28.4 per cent industry, 20.7 per cent manufacturing, and 67.3 per cent services. 12th largest economy worldwide and second in Latin America (after Brazil). In 2000, Mexico had the 9th largest crude petroleum proved reserves in the world, with 28.3 billion barrels, and was 8th in crude production, with 3.0 billion barrels daily. During 1998, Mexico ranked 9th among the leading exporters of auto and auto parts in the world, and 3rd among the suppliers for the US automotive industry. In 1999, for the 4th consecutive year, Mexico exported more than one million vehicles to world markets. During 1999 Mexican exports of auto and autoparts to the US exceeded US$ 24.2 billion, and Mexico's share in total US automotive imports grew from 7.2 per cent in 1993 to 13 per cent in 1999.
As of 1998, there were 38.6 million people employed in Mexico, of which 20.2 per cent were involved in agriculture; 24.5 per cent were involved in industry; and 54.9 per cent were involved in services; the

remainder were not specified. Mexico exported a total of US$ 166.5 billion goods (f.o.b, 2000), including assembly plant operations (*maquiladoras*). Mexico's exports consisted of 87.3 per cent manufactures (47.7 per cent of which was *maquiladoras*), 9.8 per cent oil, and 2.5 per cent agriculture, with the remainder not specified. Exports went primarily to the US (88.6 per cent) and Canada (2 per cent). Trade with the US and Canada has tripled since the implementation of NAFTA in 1994. Mexico imported a total of US$ 174.5 billion goods (c.i.f, 2000), of which 76.6 per cent was intermediate goods, 13.8 per cent was capital goods, and 9.6 per cent was consumer goods. 35.4 per cent of imports were related to the *maquiladora* industry (off shore assembly for re-export), producing a trade deficit of US$ 8 billion. The current-account deficit reached US$18.2bn, equivalent to 3.1% of GDP.

Annual foreign investment (2000) – US$12.5 billion. Of this investment, US$ 7.6 billion was in the industrial sector, US$ 2.9 billion in the services sector, US$ 1.7 billion in the trade sector, US$ 0.2 billion in the extractive sector, with the remainder in agriculture. The

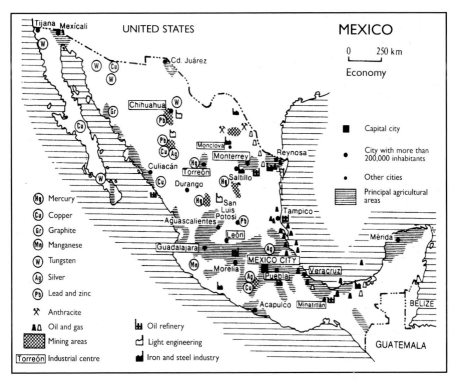

UNITED STATES

MEXICO

0   250 km

Economy

■ Capital city

● City with more than
200,000 inhabitants

• Other cities

≡ Principal agricultural
areas

(Hg) Mercury
(Cu) Copper
(Gr) Graphite
(Mn) Manganese
(W) Tungsten
(Ag) Silver
(Pb) Lead and zinc
✗ Anthracite
▲△ Oil and gas
▒ Mining areas
Torreón Industrial centre

⛏ Oil refinery
⌐ Light engineering
🏭 Iron and steel industry

US accounts for 80 per cent of all foreign investment. Total external debt outstanding and disbursed (2000) was US$154.7 billion, or 26.9 per cent of GDP. Interest payments were US$ 11.5 billion, or 2 per cent of GDP. Total debt service (2000) was US$ 63 billion (38 per cent of exported goods). Inflation in 2000 was 9.5 per cent, down from 26.7 per cent in 1990. Gross domestic savings – 21.5 per cent of GDP.

Oil: Mexico controls the second largest oil reserves (approximately 28.3 billion barrels) in the Western Hemisphere, after Venezuela. Mexico is the world's third-ranked oil exporting nation. In the first half of 1999, Mexico was the largest supplier of crude oil to the United States. Mexican oil production in 1999 reached an average of 3.37 million barrels per day (b/d), of which about 2.9 million b/d was crude oil. Crude oil production decreased slightly in 1999 from 1998 levels, following four years of increases. Mexico's oil industry is a major source (about 40%) of government revenue. Total Mexican exports were 1.5 million b/d and earned the state treasury US$10.4 billion in 2000. The United States, Spain, Netherland Antilles, and Japan are key oil export markets for Mexico. After the recovery in oil prices in 1999-2000, oil exports represented 9.8 per cent of total exports for the year 2000 as a whole.

NAFTA: NAFTA has led to increased trade flows

between Mexico, Canada and the United States. During the first seven years of its implementation, Mexico's trade with its NAFTA partners tripled, reaching US$275 billion in 2000. Mexico's trade with the US in 2000 increased 153 per cent since 1994, and trade with Canada has increased 147 per cent in the same time period. Since January 1994, trade among NAFTA partners has grown at an annual average rate of 11.8 per cent. The US is Mexico's leading source in FDI. Between 1994 and 2000, US firms have invested more than 40.3 billion dollars; 59.3 per cent in the manufacturing sector, 20.5 per cent in services, 14.2 per cent in commerce, 4.3 per cent in transport and communications and 1.7 per cent in other sectors. Canada is Mexico's fifth source in FDI. Between 1994 and September 2000, Canadian firms have invested nearly 2.8 billion dollars; 57.1 per cent in the manufacturing sector, 28.3 per cent in services, 9.1 per cent in mining and 5.0 per cent in commerce. Nevertheless, critics suggest that the promised benefits of new jobs from NAFTA, higher wages in Mexico, environmental clean-up and improved health along the border have failed to materialize. In addition, NAFTA may increase

income inequality, as high-paying manufacturing jobs, are, in the majority of cases, replaced by lower-paid employment; and industrial development focuses on northern states close to the US, widening disadvantages for the south. Government statistics indicate a third of the working population earns less than that the official US$4 a day minimum. Official figures suggest that since the 1994-95 crisis inequality has become slightly worse.

Trade and Aid relations with the US: In six years, trade between Mexico and US has more than tripled, growing at an average annual rate of 16.7 percent. As a result, today Mexico is the second largest export market for US goods, only behind Canada. In 2000, Mexico-US trade reached US$ 263.5 billion, 209.2 per cent more than the registered in 1993, the year prior to NAFTA. Mexico has increased its share in total US imports from 6.8 per cent in 1993 to 11.2 per cent during 2000. In 2000, Mexican purchased US products totalling US$ 127.6 billion, 181.6 percent more than the registered in the same period of 1993.

HISTORY AND POLITICS

Some key dates

* 1325: Aztecs settle in central Mexico and found their capital at Tenochtitlán, on the present-day site of Mexico City * 1521: Spanish *conquistador* Hernán Cortés conquers Aztec empire, initiating 300 years of Spanish rule over Mexico * 1810: Miguel Hidalgo y Costilla, a priest, proclaims Mexican independence from Spain, but is swiftly captured and executed * 1821: Conservative forces, led by former Spanish officer Agustín de Iturbide, secure Mexican independence * 1834: After years of settlement by US immigrants, Texas secedes from Mexico. Mexican General Santa Ana arrives to put down the rebellion, storms the Alamo, but is subsequently defeated by rebellious Texans. US annexes Texas * 1846: US declares war on Mexico, wins and annexes California, Nevada, Arizona, New Mexico, Utah and part of Colorado * 1860: Benito Juárez becomes first Indian president of Mexico * 1863: After dispute over debt repayments, French, Spanish and British troops invade, installing the Austrian Emperor's Brother as Emperor Maximilian I of Mexico * 1867: Juárez captures and executes Maximilian * 1876: General Porfirio Díaz seizes power

and begins 35 year dictatorship * 1910-1917: Bloody and chaotic Mexican Revolution ends in Venustiano Carranza becoming president * 1919: Carranza has peasant leader Emiliano Zapata murdered * 1929: Founding of the National Revolutionary Party (PNR), later renamed the PRI, which was still in power 67 years later * 1934: Lázaro Cárdenas becomes president, pushes through sweeping land reforms and nationalises the oil industry * 1954: Women granted the right to vote * 1968: Prior to Mexico City's hosting of the Olympics, government massacres hundreds of leftist student demonstrators at Tlatelolco * 1976: José López Portillo becomes president and uses booming oil revenues and massive foreign borrowing to fuel record period of economic growth * 1982: boom turns to bust, as Mexico is forced to suspend debt repayments, initiating Latin American debt crisis * 1985: 10,000 to 30,000 people die as Mexico City is hit by devastating earthquake * 1988: Carlos Salinas defeats former PRI heavyweight Cuauhtémoc Cárdenas (son of Lázaro) in fraudulent elections. Cárdenas had split from the PRI, setting up the National Democratic Front, the first serious electoral threat to the PRI in decades * 1992:

President Salinas and US President George Bush sign North American Free Trade Agreement (NAFTA) with Canada * 1994: NAFTA comes into effect on New Years' day, but the government's celebrations are wrecked by a peasant uprising in the southern state of Chiapas. Troops of the hitherto unknown Zapatista National Liberation Front (EZLN) seize four towns before withdrawing to their bases in the hills * March 1994: Donaldo Colosio, the PRI's presidential candidate, is assassinated in Tijuana, marking the start of a period of internal division within the previously monolithic ruling party * August 1994: Colosio's replacement Ernesto Zedillo easily defeats Cárdenas in presidential elections * December 1994: Weeks after taking office, Zedillo is forced to devalue, and the resulting exodus of foreign capital plunges Mexico into economic crisis * 1995: Despite a US$50 billion bail-out put together by Washington, the Mexican economy shrinks by 7 per cent as two million people lose their jobs in one of the worst recessions in living memory. * April 1996: Zapatistas break off talks with Zedillo government over its failure to implement an agreement to end hostilities known as the San Andres accords* December 1997:

Massacre of 45 indigenous people, mainly women and children, in the Chiapas village of Acteal by an armed group linked to local PRI bosses* July 1997: Cuauhtémoc Cárdenas of the PRD becomes first elected mayor of Mexico City, signaling declining PRI power * February 2000: Federal police end a 292-day student strike and occupation of National Autonomous University in Mexico City over plans to raise tuition* July 2000: Vicente Fox of the PAN wins the presidency, ending a 71 year-long PRI rule.* March 2001: Zapatistas stage a two-week march ending in Mexico City, where they called on Congress to approve an Indian-rights bill based on the San Andreas accords May 2001: Congress approved a watered down version of a bill granting special rights to Mexico's Indian peoples* September 2001: Recession affects Mexico's assembly plants and reduces exports, shrinking the economy 1.6 per cent in the 3rd quarter as a result of heightened US border security and recession post September 11th* October 2001: Digna Ochoa, a human rights lawyer, is murdered, raising questions of army involvement* March 2002: Former Mexico City mayor Rosario Robles elected to head the PRD under contested elections* March

2002: Mexico hosts the UN International Conference on Financing Development, where nations pledge to increase foreign aid to developing countries